RESEARCHING LANGUAGE:

English Project Work at 'A' Level and Beyond

D1513647

The Author:

Angela Goddard has taught English in a variety of schools and colleges. She ran the Language in the National Curriculum Project in Tameside, Stockport and Manchester 1990–92. Currently she is Senior Lecturer in English in the School of Education, Manchester Metropolitan University. Her publications include *The Language Awareness Project, Years 10 and 11: Language and Gender, Packs 1 and 2* (Framework Press, 1989), and with John Keen and John Shuttleworth, *English Language 'A' Level: The Starter Pack* (Framework Press, 1991). She is Project Chief Moderator for NEAB English Language 'A' level, in which capacity she has guided the development of the research project element since the inception of the course in 1983.

Editor:

Karen Westall

Acknowledgements:

Grateful thanks to all the English Language 'A' Level students who have contributed data and ideas to this book. The contributions of the following groups and individuals are also gratefully acknowledged:

Dr Alan Cruttenden, Manchester University Dept. of Linguistics, for material on intonation; LINC Working Party members: in particular, Liz Armstrong for the material on weddings; Tony Meheran for the material on the language of gravestones; Jane Hamshere and Carol Ashton for the 'birth cards' idea; Fiona Stiles, Janet Lee and Karen Moorcroft for the different versions of 'The Argument'; Mike Booth for the weather forecasts; The LINC Primary Advisory Teachers for Tameside, Stockport and Manchester, and Working Party Members: in particular, Ann Howard for transcripts of young children talking; Jan Turner for the nursery writing; Judith Chapman for 'The Tooth Fairy'; Sally Heap, English Primary Advisory Teacher for Stockport, for 'Little Bonkey'; Rob Greenall, Manchester Metropolitan University, for 'Incey Wincey Spider'.

RESEARCHING LANGUAGE:

English Project Work at 'A' Level and Beyond

Angela Goddard

First published in 1993 by
Framework Press Educational Publishers Ltd.
St Leonard's House
St Leonardgate
LANCASTER LA1 1NN

RESEARCHING LANGUAGE
English Project Work at 'A' Level and Beyond

A catalogue record for the pack is available from the
British Library

ISBN 1 85008 024 0

Cover design by John Angus

Illustrations by Lynne Dougall

Typeset by Blackpool Typesetting Services Ltd., Blackpool

Printed in Great Britain by
H. Charlesworth & Co. Ltd., Huddersfield

Table of Contents

Introduction

This book is intended to support students who are embarking on a language investigation. Although it is initially aimed at NEAB English Language 'A' Level students, and therefore occasional references are made to the rubric of that syllabus, it will also be useful to Higher Education students who, as part of a course or module, are required to undertake a piece of language research.

Teachers of related 'A' Level subjects – such as Communication Studies, or some of the wider English Literature syllabuses – and teachers in secondary schools wishing to develop more systematic Knowledge About Language work at Key Stages 3 and 4 will also find the linguistic areas and approaches to analysis outlined here a useful support to their curriculum content and delivery.

The NEAB syllabus requires students to submit their research projects towards the end of year 2 of their course, and most students write their investigations during the first two terms of that year. However, the idea of investigation is at the core of the whole course, as it should be in any course of language study, and the best practice in our schools and colleges will focus students at the outset on what investigation means, allowing them to develop their skills and knowledge by regularly working on rich data which raises interesting and varied questions about language. The principal aim of this book is to support and endorse that good practice by providing material and approaches that have been seen, through extensive trialling, to encourage active learning from the beginning.

Possible ways of working are varied and flexible: the book can be the basis of shared group work in classroom situations, with further research being undertaken independently by groups or individuals; students who are in the position of having to work alone, with only an occasional opportunity to meet with a supervisor, will also find the book useful distance learning material which teaches necessary analytical skills and provides research ideas and approaches.

The only thing this book is *not* is a handbook to be clutched at the eleventh hour by students who are looking for rescue from the tyranny of approaching deadlines.

If the book contributes to a spirit of genuine enquiry in any piece of language research, then it will have succeeded.

Working Instructions

Initial Activities provide a starting point for tackling data in particular research areas.

Further Activities develop analysis in more detail by:
— encouraging reflection on findings, guiding students towards main points or issues and relating language features to the wider social contexts of use;
— providing additional material which is designed to deepen and broaden the research outlook.

Research Pathways give suggestions for further pieces of group or independent research.

 Work as a whole group

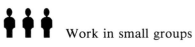

Work in small groups

 Work in pairs

 Work individually, either in classroom or in distance learning contexts

Section A

LAYING THE FOUNDATIONS

✦ ✦ ✦

4

1. What Does Researching Language Involve?

INITIAL ACTIVITY

Read through the following outline of some of the important aspects of language research. When you have finished, make notes on any points you are unclear about. Prepare to raise any of these points with your supervisor.

◆ ◆ ◆

In order to decide on a topic to research, you have to know what a piece of language research is – and isn't.

The NEAB 'A' Level English Language syllabus defines the language project as a 'Report on a personal investigation into a specified aspect of language use in everyday life', and states that you should write 2,000–4,000 words, excluding the data you collect for your research.

Language research projects for other courses may well vary in size or scope or depth of analysis, but any language investigation is likely to involve certain key factors that are described in the NEAB quote above. These are as follows:

INVESTIGATION

It's important to realise straight away that a language research project is an investigation rather than an essay.

It will involve your asking a question about a particular aspect of language, then collecting material and analysing it, in order to answer that question. That means your going out and discovering for yourself how language works, rather than taking somebody else's word for it. It means evaluating your findings, rather than arguing a point in an abstract way. It means being scientific and honest in the way you go about collecting your material. Above all, it means being open-minded, not assuming you already know all the answers, or expecting them to be neat and tidy.

All these things are the hallmark of a good piece of language research.

REPORT

Writing a report is different from doing a piece of creative writing or a discussion essay. You are not aiming simply to demonstrate your skill as a writer, or put across a point of view you already have. Your aim is to inform the reader about language by explaining your investigation and commenting on your findings.

Of course, it's very important to write clearly and simply, in order to make your reader understand what you were trying to do. But that might involve presenting your report partly in the form of a series of tables or graphs, or in any other shape that will enable you to illustrate your ideas. In the end, how you present your report is entirely up to you.

A SPECIFIED AREA

Before you go out and collect material, you need to decide on a particular area that interests you. You don't have to know this in detail – it's important to remain flexible, and willing to adapt your approach to the material you collect. But you do need to fix on a general area before you start your research. It will help you – and your supervisor – to write down a plan of what you intend to do.

For the NEAB course, there is no specified list of topics from which you must choose: any area may be investigated, provided that it has enough of a *language* focus to enable you to demonstrate your skills.

LANGUAGE USE IN EVERYDAY LIFE

The phrase 'language use' means exactly what it says – you are researching how language is actually used by people. That means, for research on spoken language, tape-recording and transcribing some real speech; while you wouldn't need to do that for the analysis of written material, you would still be looking at the same general question – how is the language being used?

PERSONAL COMMITMENT

It's important that you choose a topic you are genuinely interested in. If you are interested, you will be committed to seeing the project through to the end; your perseverance will result in a thorough analysis of your chosen material; and your enthusiasm will be evident to any reader. All these qualities will result in a more satisfying experience for you, because you will be creating a piece of work you are proud of; and they will gain you many marks in the final assessment.

It's natural for you to think of your supervisor as the reader for whom you are writing, since that person will be your first reader and the marker of your work. But it's best not to think that way. Your work should be understandable to any interested general reader, and you should aim to make that reader want to follow you on your chosen investigation. Fix on a person you know would fit that category, and aim your report at him/her.

If your project is going to interest anyone else, then it must be something that engages you and stretches you a bit. It must be something that will keep your interest for quite a long time, so it's important to take on a challenge rather than settle for a 'safe bet' to which you think you already know all the answers. Again, you'll be rewarded in the final assessment for choosing something challenging, even if the end result is imperfect.

But the problem is this: how do you know what you're interested in?

The best starting place for any language researcher on the lookout for a case is close to home. *Unit 2* will help you to assess your own credentials as a researcher.

2. Reviewing Your Credentials

The following questionnaire is designed to make you start thinking about the language resources that you have around you.

INITIAL ACTIVITY I

Complete the questionnaire. If you are working in pairs discuss each item with your partner, then write down your individual answers in a study file or notebook.

QUESTIONNAIRE

i) *Your Own Language Development*

Make a list of anything you still have in your possession that relates to your own language development. Here are some examples:

School exercise books	Old comics or magazines
Early readers	Tape-recordings of you
Teachers' Reports	Old diaries, scrapbooks or other notebooks

ii) *Your Family*

Write down some details in note form in response to the following questions:

Do you have younger relatives who are at the early stages of learning language?

Do the people in your immediate family use a particular accent, dialect, or know more than one language?

Is there anyone in your family who has had particular language problems?

Do you have relatives who work in occupations that use a specific type of language?

Do the older members of your family have any collections of particular types of material (e.g. football programmes, greetings cards)?

Do you think you use language differently from your older relatives? If so, how?

Do particular family members fall into certain 'roles' in group conversations (e.g. peacemaker, agitator, listener)?

---

continued

Questionnaire continued

---

iii) *You Now*

Do you belong to any groups or take part in any leisure activities that have their own forms of language?

Do you do any part-time work that involves you in using language in a certain way?

Do you collect, read and/or write particular sorts of material?

Do any of your friends have particular accents and dialects, or use more than one language? (e.g. Do you have any foreign penfriends?)

iv) *And Your Addictions*

What kind of an addict are you?

What are some of the things that fascinate you about the language you see and hear around you?

For example, are you interested in any of the types of language set out below? Choose *three* items from the list, or make up your own list of *three* types of language that particularly intrigue you, and try to decide what it is about them that fascinates you.

The conversations people have on buses or trains	People's names
	Advertising tricks
The way people speak on the telephone, or to answering machines	Persuasive speeches
	Body language
	Certain types of literature
Problem pages in magazines	Junk mail
Shop names	Car names
Road signs	Gravestones
Sign language	The way other languages work
Graffiti	Song lyrics
Ritual language used in ceremonies, e.g. weddings, funerals	Personal (small ads) columns
	Job jargon
	Bias in the Press
Greetings	The way animals communicate
Terms of address	Children's expressions

◆ ◆ ◆

INITIAL ACTIVITY II or

If you are working individually, make notes on your initial ideas, in preparation for your next meeting with your supervisor.

If you are working as a whole group, each person should choose *one* aspect of his/her notes to report back on to the rest of the group. Set a deadline for all group members to bring in a piece of material that relates to some aspect of their notes. Each member of the group should then give a five minute presentation on this material, explaining its source and what it indicates about the chosen aspect(s) of language.

◆ ◆ ◆

3. What Do You Know?

As a language user, you already know a great deal about language. How can you convert what you know implicitly, as a language user, into conscious knowledge which can form the basis of an analysis? This unit is going to help you answer that question.

Decoding Written Texts

Readers – even very young ones – bring a lot of knowledge of different aspects of language to the decoding of written texts.

Reading is not simply recognising individual words; it is understanding how texts are put together, how they work. Good readers have an awareness of a specific number of language areas or *levels*.

LANGUAGE LEVEL I: GRAPHOLOGY

Graphology – which literally means 'the study of marks' – refers to all the visual aspects of written language. So aspects like layout, typeface, punctuation, spelling, abbreviations, images and other artwork such as logos would be included here.

Don't be confused by the fact that, outside the area of Linguistics, the term 'graphology' is used to refer narrowly to the study of handwriting.

INITIAL ACTIVITY

Look at the differently shaped texts on p.10.

Imagine that the horizontal lines are lines of writing.

How do the different layouts give you an indication of how these texts should be read, and what they are?

(Suggested answers on p.12.)

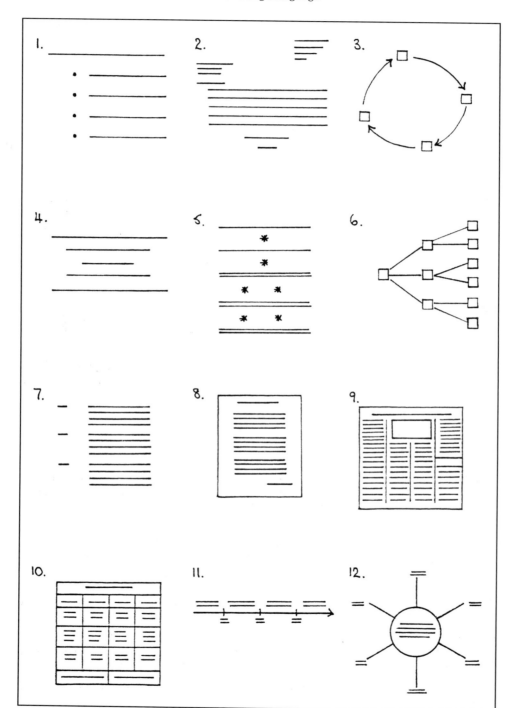

When you have finished, go on to look at the data below. What *graphological* devices are being used in these texts, and what meanings are being conveyed in each case?

> Deceptively spac. gr fl flat,
> nicely dec. th'out, full gas ch,
> comm. gdns, gge, entryphone.

The Dead

You Are Invited to a Party

With Deepest Sympathy

If you were working in small groups in a class situation, report back your findings to the whole group. If you were working alone, make some written notes for your own reference.

✦ ✦ ✦

FURTHER ACTIVITY 👤 or 👤👤👤

If you are working in groups, look through a range of magazines and newspapers to find 10–15 symbols and logos. These do not have to be from adverts – they could be from small ads pages, magazine features, etc. Cut them out and paste them onto a sheet.

Make sure you don't give your readers any clues about where they've come from (i.e. by including brand-names for adverts), and try not to make them too obvious.

Make a note yourselves of their source. Number the cuttings.

When you have finished, swap your sheets around, so that each group is given another's cuttings.

Each group should then write down their associations for each symbol or logo – what does it remind them of? Even if they know where the cuttings are from, they should try to say what image, idea or feeling they are given by each cutting.

Compare all the results with the answers, pin up all the sheets for everyone to see and discuss the following questions:

- Can you find any patterns in how symbols and logos are used?

- Are certain types of symbol used in our culture to suggest particular ideas?

- If any members of the group have knowledge of other cultures or societies, are there any symbols or images used there to suggest different ideas?

If you are working individually, make a collection of different types of symbols and logos and write down the details as above. If possible, find six informants and ask them what associations they have for each symbol or logo.

Try to find patterns in how the symbols and logos are used, and in what people's associations are.

When you have finished, keep all your material as a reminder of what this language level is all about.

ANSWERS (INITIAL ACTIVITY p.9)

1. An information text where a piece of information is given and then expanded on in a number of 'bullet points'.

2. A letter.

3. A diagram where information is read in a clockwise direction; each piece of information relies on (i.e. is causally related to) the preceding piece.

4. This could be an ornamental plaque, e.g. a gravestone inscription, or a concrete poem, where the shape made by the lines represents an object or idea in the real world.

5. A menu.

6. Information is read left to right; the boxes to the right in each case expand on those to the left.

7. A text where information is marked off in sections which are all equal in status (unlike No. 1, where the bullet points are equal to each other but secondary in status to the line at the top), e.g. the TV listings in a newspaper.

8. A poem.

9. A newspaper.

10. A tabulation.

11. A time-line, read from left to right, with information about each stage of the chronology.

12. Information set in a thematic structure: a summary of the subject in the centre, with subsections marked at radial points. The pieces of information on the 'spokes' do not rely on each other, as in No. 3.

LANGUAGE LEVEL II: PHONOLOGY

Phonology refers to the study of sound.

It may seem strange to think of considering sound in written language, but writers know that readers use an 'inner ear' when reading texts; sound patterns may also correspond to visual (i.e. letter) patterns, traceable by the eye. Manipulating patterns of sound can make a text more memorable; the use of devices such as rhyme, alliteration, and the use of puns which rely on sound, or playing sound off against spelling, are the staple of advertising copywriters. Writers of 'serious' texts are unlikely to use sound patterning extensively, because this can lead to a sense of lightheartedness and playfulness – as in tonguetwisters, rhyming jingles and jokes.

INITIAL ACTIVITY

Look at the data below. What *phonological* devices are being used in these texts, and what is their purpose?

TABLOID HEADLINE: **Big, bronze Buddha bagged by burglars**

HAIRDRESSERS' SHOP NAMES:

The Hairport	Hairazors
Fellaz Hair Design	Classic Cutz
Aries	Tint Inn
The Men's Den	

COCKTAIL NAMES:

Cocktails

Singin' in the Rhein

Go in Seine

Czech Mate

Nothing Toulouse

Barbara Seville

If you were working in small groups, report back your findings to the whole group. If you were working individually, make some written notes for your own reference.

◆ ◆ ◆

FURTHER ACTIVITY

Look through a range of tabloid newspapers for uses of phonological devices. If you are working in groups, one group should look for rhyme; one group for uses of sound symbolism (sometimes called 'onomatopoeia' – where the word imitates a sound); two or more groups should look for uses of alliteration. The groups searching for alliteration might decide to concentrate on particular sounds.

Cut out all your examples.

If you find a feature which may be useful to another group, offer it to them for their collection.

When you have finished, paste your examples onto some display sheets, and pin them up for everyone to see. Invent a title for your display, then discuss the following questions:

● How far does the tabloid press play on sound to achieve certain effects in the language used?

● What effects are created, in your opinion?

If you are working individually, categorise your extracts, and try to answer the questions above.

LANGUAGE LEVEL III: SEMANTICS

This refers to the choice of words and phrases which, put together, weave a pattern of meaning. Many different aspects of language choice could be significant here, for example:

the level of formality – use of colloquial language, or abstract, Latin-based vocabulary (e.g. have a go/try/endeavour kick-off/begin/commence);

the field of reference – terms that are all from the same area of knowledge or experience (e.g. medicine, computers, love, war);

connotation – the way in which some words and phrases can evoke powerful association or feelings in the reader's mind, and make him/her view the subject matter in a certain light (e.g. freedom fighter/terrorist). Foreign terms are sometimes used to give particular impressions, playing on the stereotypes we have of different cultures (e.g. French 'romance' to sell perfume; German 'efficiency' to market cars);

the use of idiomatic language – language that works on more than the simply literal level (e.g. metaphor, pun). Idiomatic language can be put to a variety of uses; often it works towards constructing a particular viewpoint for the reader, sometimes by bringing different ideas together in a new way;

collocation – the way in which certain items of language are expected to occur together, and in a certain order (e.g. fish and chips; he and she; Father, Son and Holy Ghost). Some collocations become cliches – rather worn-out and empty phrases (e.g. blushing bride; rack and ruin; come rain or shine);

language change – terms can die out, suggest a bygone age (be 'archaic'), be new coinages (neologisms), narrow or widen their meanings, or go up and down in respectability. Sensitivity to these changes is one of the ways we can date a text.

INITIAL ACTIVITY 🚹 or 🚹🚹🚹

Look at the data on pp.15–17. What *semantic* devices are being used in these texts, and what meanings are conveyed by them?

GUARDIAN

hester   **Wednesday August 15 1984   23p**

Jubilant West Indies supporters spelt out their thoughts (above) after England's defeat yesterday while Joel Garner (below) grabbed a couple of souvenirs of his six-wicket tally in the match.   Picture above by Frank Martin

First published in *The Guardian* (Frank Martin)

INNER SOUND AND VOICE WORKSHOPS, 1992

Among the Activities We Will Share:

- We will learn Mongolian overtone chanting, an ancient shamanic vocal practice which makes audible the natural harmonic spectrum of the voice in its pure rainbow colours, so that unearthly, angelic and bell-like tones are heard floating above the voices of the chanters.

- We will learn vocal purification practices and how to cleanse the chakras and subtle body.

- We will explore sonorous yogas and vocal practices involving the elements.

- We will explore, in order to forgive and clear, the patterns of our ancestral lines.

HAIRDRESSERS' SHOP NAMES:

Power Cuts   Room at the Top
The Head Gardener   Headmasters
Blade Runners   A Head Start
As You Like It   Cuts Bothways

TOILET CISTERN NAMES:

The Little Niagara
The Great Athenaeum
The Dauntless Bi-Flow
The Avalanche

NEWSPAPER HEADLINES:

Nurses Upset by Cuts
Fireman Marries Old Flame
Mothers Who Smoke Have Lighter Children
Butter Price War Spreads

CAR NAMES:

Escort Estate, Fiesta, Metro City
Maestro, Rover, Sierra, Cavalier
Scirocco, Polo, Golf Clubman

CAFE LA MAISON

Specials
A tournedos of beef topped with a liver parfait,
enrobed in crepinette and oven baked,
served with a Madeira and truffle fondue
escorted by pommes sautes aux fines herbes
★ ★ ★ ★ ★ ★ ★

On my way out I knocked at Mr. Contreras's door. He was inside again and much relieved to see me. I let his waves of information about the glazier wash over me, thanking him when there was a break in the surf, then explaining my going back out.

Sara Paretsky: *Guardian Angel*

HERE
Lies in a horizontal position
the outside case of
THOMAS HINDE
Clock and watch maker,
Who departed this life
Wound up in hope
Of being taken in hand
By his Maker,
And being thoroughly cleaned,
Repaired and set a-going,
In the world to come,
On the 15th of August, 1830,
In the 19th Year of his Age.

Read through the penfriend's letter on p.18.

What aspects of English semantics are giving this writer some problems?

If you were working in small groups, feed back your results to the whole group. If you were working individually, make some written notes on your findings, as a summary for your own use.

✦ ✦ ✦

Via N. Furnari n.° 45,
89100 Reggio CALABRIA
ITALIA

Dear Diane,

I also like you, I have been very busy, I am busy still. I am studing for University, I must study for two examinations for April and besides the Language and Literature English and Language and Literature Spanish for June. But the truth problem is the english language. I love it, but I have a Professor very crazy. Your name is Bernard Dold, he is of Liverpool.

This year St. Valentine's day has been ugly because my boyfriend there isn't. He is making the military service. However also we use to send the cards to our boyfriends. Besides also we use presents, or a candlelight meal, or flowers.

I am happy because in short days will be my birthday: 31th March, I am 21. I am old! When is your birthday? Excuse me but I have forgotten it.

My boyfriend's name is Carmelo. I have been going-out with him five years.

How are you? I hope well and I hope well also for your ill friends.   By for now

P.S. WRITE SOON, PLEASE—   love Maria

CIAO!

N.B— I haven't understand the word "going-out". It mean to go out, or to get engaged-? Please, write me correct form—.

FURTHER ACTIVITY I: Metaphor or

Many of the everyday terms we use are metaphorical, but we use them so often that we often don't realise this. Look at the examples below:

I laughed my head off;   he cried his eyes out;   I nearly died laughing;   button your lip;   I'm in a hurry – must fly!;   her eyes were glued to the TV set;   he broke my heart;   I'm going out of my mind;   pull yourself together;   shake a leg;   pull your socks up;   our eyes met across the room;   keep your nose out of my affairs . . .

Sometimes it is possible to group a number of sayings together, as variations on one basic metaphor. For example:

Love as a Journey

We've come to the parting of the ways. You need to go your way, and I'll go mine.

We've come to a crossroads in our relationship. We've come a long way together, but this is the end of the road. Maybe in a while our paths will cross again . . .

Argument as Warfare

She shot my argument down in flames. My argument was riddled with holes. We clashed, fought head-on, she attacked me and won. I had no back-up at all. She marshalled all her forces and ambushed me. I surrendered, and we called a truce . . .

Now take one of the metaphors below, and brainstorm all the terms you can think of, along the lines of *Love as a Journey* and *Argument as Warfare*:

A Lover as Food   Anger as a Boiling Liquid
Words as Weapons   Emotions as Colours
The Brain as a Machine   Time as Money
Anger as Fire

If you have been working in groups, share your ideas with the whole group and discuss the following questions:

● Are there further metaphors you can think of, that are used in everyday conversations?

● Do you think that having metaphors such as the above conditions us to think in a certain way?

● What would be the difference in our way of thinking if we had the following metaphors?

A Lover as a Building   The Brain as a Flower
Words as Smells

Try making up some sayings, to see what these ideas would sound like.

✦ ✦ ✦

FURTHER ACTIVITY II: Levels of Formality or

In English, you can express the same idea in a number of different ways, depending on how formal or informal you want to sound. For example, how would you ask where the toilet was in the following contexts?

Asking your interviewer, at an interview
Asking a stranger in a pub
Asking your best friend in a disco or club

Different levels of formality in English are often related to foreign loan words: French- or Latin-based words are often more formal than Anglo-Saxon words. Here are some examples:

French/Latin origin	*Anglo-Saxon origin*
perspire	sweat
expire	die
desist	stop

Now read through the following passages, which are three accounts of the same incident. The passages represent three different levels of formality, or styles:

• A very informal style containing lots of slang and dialect (from the Manchester area)

• An average Standard English style

• A highly formal Standard English style

Read the passages aloud.

THE BARNEY

T'other day there were a barney at paper shop between Mr Arnold Higginbottom and Mrs Nora Grimshaw. Mr Higginbottom had been chunnerin' on about Mrs Grimshaw's two kids who'd been playing footy in the entry and gawping over his fence when they lost their ball.

Anyroad, Mrs Grimshaw were gobsmacked about this. She said, 'What ya' mitherin' about, ya' lemon? Why are ya' gettin' so nowty?' He said that he'd just legged it back from t' factory and he were feeling dead powfagged and he were pig sick of them moping about his yard. He said she should of leathered 'em in the first place and she'd better tell them if they did it again they'd get done.

She said that if it came to complaints, she had a few of her own. His moggy had been messing in her spud patch and had been scratting around there for weeks.

He told her to put a sock in it, and upped and went out of the shop. He barged into an old bid what were trying to come in, knocked his hat off of his head and shoved him to the ground. The old codger started whingeing straight away and were carted off to the hospital where they gave him a full check-up. He were shook up and flapping, but apart from a sore lug'ole he were sorted, so they give him a brew and sent him off home for a kip.

THE ARGUMENT

The other day, there was an argument at the newsagent's between Mr Arnold Higginbottom and Mrs Nora Grimshaw. Mr Higginbottom had been complaining about Mrs Grimshaw's two children who had been playing football in the alleyway and staring over his fence when they lost their ball.

Anyway, Mrs Grimshaw was surprised about this. She said, 'What are you complaining about, you silly man? Why are you getting so cross?' He said he had just hurried back from the factory and he was feeling really tired and he was very fed up with them hanging around in his yard. He said she should have smacked them in the first place and she had better tell them that if they did it again, they would be punished by him.

She said that if it came to complaints, she had a few of her own. His cat had been digging in her potato patch and had been scratching around there for weeks.

He told her to be quiet and left the shop. He bumped into an old man who was trying to come in, knocked his hat off his head and pushed him to the ground. The old man started complaining at once, and was taken to the hospital where they gave him a full check-up. He was very shaken and flustered, but apart from a sore ear he was all right, so he was given a cup of tea and sent home for a nap.

THE ALTERCATION

Recently, there was a fracas at the newsagent's between Mr Arnold Higginbottom and Mrs Nora Grimshaw. Mr Higginbottom had been levelling accusations about Mrs Grimshaw's two offspring who had been engaged in certain team games in the communal passageway and looking fixedly over his fence when they mislaid their ball.

Notwithstanding, Mrs Grimshaw was absolutely incredulous at this. She retorted, 'What is the basis of your grievance, you asinine nincompoop? Why are you becoming so irate?' He responded by stating that he had just returned post-haste from the manufacturing establishment and he was feeling utterly fatigued and he was extremely disgruntled to find them loitering on his property. He said that she should have thoroughly reprimanded them at the outset and he would be obliged if she would communicate the fact that if they persisted in their activities they would be chastised by him.

Her riposte on the subject of grievances was that, in point of fact, she had a number of objections herself. His feline companion had been unearthing her King Edwards and had been disturbing the terrain for some time. He asked her to desist and made his departure from the premises. He collided with an elderly citizen who was attempting to enter, causing his millinery to be dislodged and jostling him to the ground. The old gentleman expostulated immediately and was accompanied to the infirmary where a thorough examination was conducted upon him. He was extremely tremulous and palpitating, but aside from an injured auditory organ he was in a satisfactory condition, so he was offered a hot beverage and was despatched homewards to rest and recuperate.

What different impressions do you get of the person telling the story, from the differences in language used? How did it feel to read or listen to the accounts – for example, were the passages read in particular accents?

Try to pick out:

— dialect words and phrases from the first passage that help to give the account an informal, local flavour;

— words and phrases from the third passage that help to make the passage sound very formal (and comical in this case, because the incident would not normally be described in such a high-flown way).

◆ ◆ ◆

FURTHER ACTIVITY III   or

In the jumble of words below there are 38 pairs which have the same or similar meanings (synonyms). Try to match up these pairs: each pair has an informal sounding word (from Anglo-Saxon/Viking languages) and a formal version (from French/Latin languages). Arrange the words in two columns under the headings:

Anglo-Saxon/Viking Words (informal)   *French/Latin Words* (formal)

snag	employment	smelly	endure
meet	offensive	casserole	attire
trousers	sweat	living room	know-how
friendly	worker	residence	job
odorous	make	clothes/togs	encounter
preserve	assignment	loving	keep
cuisine	date	house	stew
talk	employee	drink	underwear
amicable	occupation	give out	manufacture
perspire	expertise	lounge	kecks
melodious	converse	task	imbibe
commence	speed up	graveyard	launder
die	disseminate	work	booze
assistance	lingerie	impediment	cookery
meeting	rude	expire	amorous
accelerate	wash	cemetery	start
put up with	driver	alcohol	help
intoxicated	coiffure	tuneful	appointment
hair-do	rendezvous	drunk	chauffeur

(Answers are on p.23.)

When you have finished, use some of these words to write two accounts of the same incident: make one version very informal – include some dialect terms – and the other version very formal. Be prepared to read your different versions out to the whole group, if you are working in a class situation.

◆ ◆ ◆

LANGUAGE LEVEL IV: GRAMMAR

This level relates to the structural patterns or 'rules' that any language has, in order to relate items to each other. If you imagine language as a wall, then the words and phrases are bricks, and the grammar is the cement that holds them together in certain patterns. Different walls – different languages – are patterned in slightly different ways.

Young children learn grammatical patterns along with vocabulary and sounds at a very early age; your own knowledge of grammar will be extensive in terms of your *use* of language, although you might not be able to analyse the structures you use in an abstract way.

There are many different aspects of grammar which could contribute to meaning in a text. Below are some of the aspects of grammar that it might be useful to consider as a starting point.

Verb tense – Although writers may vary the tense of the verbs they use for reasons of style, certain types of writing tend to use particular tenses as their norm. For example, narratives often use the past tense (I came, I saw, I conquered); generalised descriptions often use the present tense (The whale is the largest living mammal); predictions, such as horoscopes and weather forecasts, often rely on constructions that suggest possibility, probability or certainty (words like 'may', 'could' and 'will').

Answers (Further Activity III p.22)

Synonyms

Anglo-Saxon/ Viking Words (informal)	French/Latin Words (formal)	Anglo-Saxon/ Viking Words (informal)	French/Latin Words (formal)
snag	impediment	cookery	cuisine
work	employment	date	appointment
smelly	odorous	talk	converse
put up with	endure	drink	imbibe
meet	encounter	underwear	lingerie
rude	offensive	job	occupation
stew	casserole	give out	disseminate
clothes/togs	attire	tuneful	melodious
kecks	trousers	start	commence
sweat	perspire	speed up	accelerate
living room	lounge	graveyard	cemetery
know-how	expertise	wash	launder
friendly	amicable	die	expire
worker	employee	booze	alcohol
house	residence	help	assistance
make	manufacture	meeting	rendezvous
keep	preserve	driver	chauffeur
task	assignment	drunk	intoxicated
loving	amorous	hair-do	coiffure

Word order – In English, certain types of words have to precede others. For example, single adjectives usually have to go in front of nouns (there are exceptions where phrases have been borrowed from other languages e.g. 'court martial', from French). Word order can also be manipulated, to a certain extent, to emphasise particular elements. For example, if writers want an item in a sentence to stand out, they will sometimes try to put it at the end, which is a point that we notice particularly – this is called the *focus* position.

Modification – This refers to the way that words and phrases can be added to others to build up descriptive information, for example, adding adjectives and adjective phrases to give further information about nouns (e.g. a tall, Victorian *building* with rotting gutters).

When items go before the noun, this is called *pre-modification*. When they go after it, this is called *post-modification*.

Sentence types – Different sentence types fulfil different functions. For example, a set of instructions will rely on command sentences (sometimes called *imperatives*), whose function is to give orders; a report may use many statement sentences (sometimes called *declaratives*) to convey facts; a piece of persuasive writing may ask the reader questions, to get him/her thinking (*interrogative* sentences) or use exclamations (*exclamatory* sentences) to express certain feelings and attitudes.

Omission of items – Certain types of writing may involve the omission of some parts of sentences. For example, newspaper headlines often omit the articles 'a' and 'the'.

Grammatical conversions – This refers to the way one type of word can be used as another, for example:

nouns can become verbs: a parent → to parent a child
verbs can become nouns: to eat → let's have some eats
adjectives can become nouns: comic → a comic
nouns can become adjectives: Berlin → the Berlin Wall
verbs can become adjectives: I must see that film → it's a must-see film

These sorts of constructions are characteristic of American English. They are a creative source of new language, and can often be found in literary and media texts.

INITIAL ACTIVITY 👤 or 👤👤👤

Look at the data below, and try to answer the questions attached.

NEWSPAPERS

a) What makes these headlines ambiguous?

GIANT WAVES DOWN TUNNEL
(article about the flooding of the cross-channel tunnel)
OLD TRAFFORD NURSE ATTACKED
GENERAL FLIES BACK TO FRONT
NINE YEARS FOR DROWNING BABY

b) Why is this headline difficult to understand?

**FERGIE: YARD PROBE POOL
SNAPS WITH TEXAN**

c) What technique is being used in these newspaper articles?

Olympic hopeful Tracey
Childline founder Esther Rantzen
Tragic film star Diana Dors' husband
Wham star George Michael's girlfriend Pat Hermandez
The Daily Mail Fun Bridge Weekends
Roald Dahl's actress-turned-writer daughter Tessa, 34
Former world motor-racing champ James Hunt

ADVERTISEMENTS

What techniques are being used in the following?

(Boddington's Beer) If You Don't Get Boddies, You'll Just Get Bitter

(Kenco Coffee) Everything We Know About Coffee, in an Instant

LITERATURE

This extract is the opening page of a children's book called *The Piggy Book*, by Anthony Browne.

The book is about sexism, and features a family where the mother is very downtrodden. How is that message put across by the grammar of this extract, as well as the vocabulary?

'Mr Piggott lived with his two sons, Simon and Patrick,
in a nice house, with a nice garden,
and a nice car in the nice garage.
Inside the house was his wife.'

INSTRUCTIONS

What grammatical features are noticeable in these different types of instructions?

Computer Manual

If your computer system does cause interference to radio or television reception, try one or more of the following measures:

- Turn the TV or radio antenna until the interference stops

- Move the computer to one side or other of the TV or radio

- Move the computer further away from the TV or radio

- Plug the computer into an outlet that is on a different circuit from the TV or radio

Knitting Pattern

Cast on 53 [53:58] sts with No. 10 needles. Work 11 rows rib as for lower edge.

Next Row: P1[1:5], *p.2, inc in next st, rep from *to last 1[1:5] sts, p to end 70[70:74] sts. Change to No. 8 needles. Work 6 rows, having 3[3:5] sts each end of needle in d.m.st, and central 64sts in patt. as Back from *to**. Working extra sts in d.m.st, inc at both ends of next and every 6th row following until there are 96[102:106] sts. Proceed to 19 inches, ending after a wrong side row.

Recipe (Holiday Confetti Bread)

1 cup milk	¼ cup lukewarm water
½ cup sugar	2 eggs, well beaten
1½ tsps salt	4 cups sifted all-purpose flour
6 tblsps butter	1½ cups mixed candied fruits, cut into small pieces
1 tsp lemon peel	½ tsp allspice
½ tsp ginger	½ cup slivered almonds
1 package active dry yeast	2 tblsps flour

Scald milk; add sugar, salt, butter and spices. Cool to lukewarm. Dissolve yeast in water. Stir in beaten eggs and milk mixture. Add the 4 cups flour and stir until moistened. Cover and set in warm place and let rise until double in bulk, about 1½ hours. Dredge fruit with the 2 tablespoons flour. Add fruit and almonds to batter; beat 2 minutes. Push into greased 2-quart mould. Set in warm place and let rise until double in bulk, about 1 hour. Bake in 350 F oven 1 hour. Makes 1 loaf.

ENGLISH AS A FOREIGN LANGUAGE

Look again at the penfriend's letter on p.18.

What aspects of English grammar is the writer having problems with?

If you have been working in small groups, share your findings with the whole group. If you have been working individually, make some notes on your findings for your file.

◆ ◆ ◆

LANGUAGE LEVEL V: DISCOURSE

The discourse level of language refers to all the larger questions you may want to ask about any piece of written data – questions like the following:

- What type of text is this?
- Where has it come from?
- What is this text for?
- Who wrote it?
- Who is it aimed at?
- How old is it?

As readers, we come to conclusions about the questions above by adding up all the clues that you have been studying in this section. The next activity will show this in action.

INITIAL ACTIVITY

Read the extracts that follow, with all the different language levels in mind:

Graphology ; Phonology ; Semantics ; Grammar ; Discourse .

Write down some notes on what is distinctive, or worthy of comment, about the extracts from the point of view of each language level.

(Notes on each of the extracts are given on pp.30–33.)

9.25 THIS HOUSE POSSESSED

> This movie spooky has a plot corny: sensitive nurse Sheila gets bad vibes in the mountain mansion where she's helping rock star Gary to get over his breakdown, and a series of sinister incidents convinces her that the place is alive. Lisa Eilbacher and Parker Stevenson are the cut-off couple, with Slim Pickens as the singer's manager. Hollywood veteran Joan Bennett as the old dear who knows what it's all about. Made in 1981. (*The Guardian* TV listings)

INVENTORY

    you left me
            nothing but nail
            parings orange peel
            empty nutshells half filled
            ashtrays dirty
            cups with dregs of
            nightcaps an odd hair
            or two of yours on my
            comb gap toothed
            bookshelves and a
            you shaped
            depression in my pillow.
                            Liz Lochhead

OXFAM ADVERT

The following was the outside cover of a flyer which arrived inside a Sunday newspaper supplement in 1986 and its aim was to persuade the reader to give money. The inside text (included on p.29) was a newspaper-style page outlining some of the preventative, self-help work being supported by the Oxfam organisation. For the purposes of this activity, analyse the cover only. The inside text has been included in order to show the text in its entirety, and you may wish to work further on the whole text at a later date. The information, expression and imagery used are not necessarily ones Oxfam would use today.

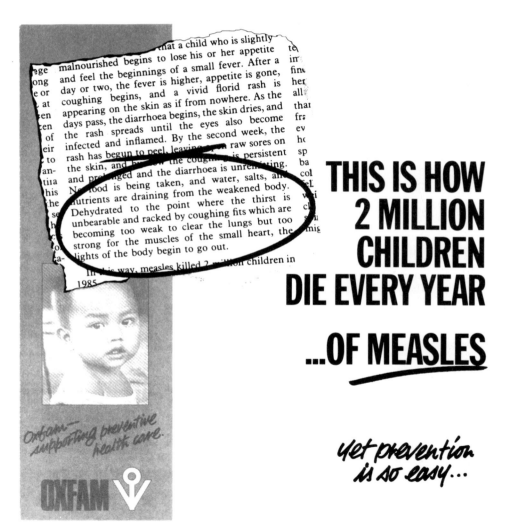

◆ ◆ ◆

3½ million children die each year from six preventable diseases; 4 million more are left disabled, blind or retarded.

Yet it takes less than £3.48 to immunise a child against these killer diseases — plus the will to make it happen.

Six diseases we know how to prevent.

Measles. Diphtheria. Whooping cough. Tetanus. Polio. TB.

The six major killer diseases that threaten two-thirds of the world's children.

- Measles accounts for 10% of all pre-school deaths in India.
- Tetanus killed nearly 1 million babies in 1985.
- Polio could disable as many as 2.5 million children over the next ten years.

The Emergency Immunisation Kit

This innovative Emergency Immunisation Kit is being developed by Oxfam, the World Health Organisation and the United Nations High Commissioner for Refugees. A powerful weapon in the fight against the six killer diseases, it enables vaccines to be kept at stable temperatures on long, difficult journeys to remote communities, so that thousands of volunteer health workers can become effective agents in immunisation programmes.

The death toll can be reduced.

Because immunisation can prevent six major killer diseases. And because in many of the poorest countries around the world, governments are encouraging local health workers, traditional midwives and parents of children in the communities at risk to join forces with health professionals in the fight against preventable disease through immunisation.

The battle has begun

In Burkina Faso, one of the poorest countries of the Sahel region of Africa, measles kills half of all the children who die between the ages of one and four.

Yet, through a massive co-ordinated effort, the people of Burkina Faso succeeded in vaccinating 1 million of their children in one three-week period. And they have taken a huge step forward in the new self-help approach to medicine known as Primary Health Care. In Burkina Faso, Oxfam's role was to fund the first training course for 25 village Health Workers and 25 midwives.

Health through self-help

This is how primary health care works. Local people choose their own Village Health Worker, often a traditional midwife, who is then trained in basic hygiene, nutrition, vaccination, and mother and child care. Back in the village, the Health Worker, with support from health services, begins a process of self-diagnosis by the community, beginning with simple health checklists.

Understanding of preventive health measures is gradually improved and good health and hygiene practices become accepted in the community

Villagers learn how vaccination prevents diseases which kill, blind and disable; how breast-feeding is the best way to nourish babies and protect them from disease; how a child can be saved from dying of diarrhoea and dehydration with just a spoonful of salt or sugar in water or a sachet of oral rehydration salts costing pence).

Support the training of Village Health Workers in their fight against the six deadly diseases.

In many parts of the developing world, women are the agents of change — it is they who will promote a new understanding of good health practice. Improved family health is the beginning of an upward spiral.

Give a mother the chance to save her children from disease and she will seize it. Once her children are healthy she will have more time, more energy and more determination to work to improve her family's lot; to spare her daughters time for education; to build a better future for them all.

Primary Health Care works

Primary Health Care emphasises prevention. It works because simple good health practices are easy to promote at community level. It costs relatively little but it provides a real basis for long-term family health.

In Burkina Faso, those first trainee health workers were pioneers.

But there are many similar initiatives springing up all over Africa, Asia and Latin America

Wherever it supports health projects around the world, Oxfam promotes the new Primary Health Care philosophy. Help us contribute to better health in developing countries through this simple but highly effective self-help approach.

Help us stop measles killing children.

As you read this, a child is dying every eight seconds from one of the six preventable diseases. Yet £3.48 will protect a child from all six.

NOTES ON EXTRACTS (INITIAL ACTIVITY p.27)

Film Review: 'This House Possessed'

Graphology:

The graphological aspects of this extract are characteristic of the television page of a newspaper: the extract is in column form, with the title of the film in heavy type, in upper case lettering, and on a line of its own. The lines of the text are indented, and are relatively short, following the general convention of news columns.

Grammar:

The grammar of this extract deviates from the norm of Standard English usage in several respects. In the first sentence, the two adjectives 'spooky' and 'corny' follow the nouns that they modify, which is a reversal of the pattern that we expect. This pattern imitates that of the title of the film, for the purpose of humour. The humorous tone of the writing is reinforced by the way in which it approaches the informality of note-form in its grammar, particularly where the characters appearing in the film are listed. Minor sentences (sentences with no main verb) at the end give the impression that the writer is anxious to get to the end of the writing task: 'Hollywood veteran Joan Bennett as the old dear who knows what it's all about. Made in 1981'. The listing accompanies omission of the article 'a' to begin with ('sensitive nurse Sheila'; 'rock star Gary'), which suggests lack of individuality, and the use of 'the' later ('the cut-off couple'; 'the old dear') which suggests that the items are ingredients to be found universally, in every such film (the use of 'the' in this way is termed 'generic').

Modification is also used extensively, to imitate tabloid style: 'sensitive nurse Sheila'; 'rock star Gary'; 'Hollywood veteran Joan Bennett'; 'the cut-off couple'.

Phonology:

There is extensive use of alliteration, which creates a playful, humorous effect: 'sensitive nurse Sheila'; 'mountain mansion'; 'series of sinister incidents'; 'cut-off couple'.

Semantics:

Many of the words and phrases used are colloquial, slang-like and sound out of date: for example, 'spooky', 'corny', 'old dear', 'knows what it's all about', 'the place is alive', 'cut-off couple'. 'Bad vibes' sounds like bygone 'hippy' language. The use of 'old dear' is particularly noticeable, carrying the connotation that the character is harmless but doddering – like the film itself. The worn-out vocabulary carries the message that the film plot is also very worn out, to the point of being comical without intending to be so.

Discourse:

All the language features noted add up to the fact that the writer finds the film particularly uninspiring – stereotyped, predictable, and dull. The choice of cliched language, the use of alliteration, and the grammatical structures noted serve to send the film up by creating an ironic, tired-sounding style.

Poem: Inventory

Graphology:

The lines are very short and list-like; there is no punctuation except a full stop at the very end; one line stands alone at the beginning. There is a title, and an author's name. If the poem had conventional punctuation, there would be commas after each item: for example, nothing but nail parings, orange peel . . . However, a list – such as a shopping list – would not have commas, necessarily. There is a link here with the title, 'Inventory'. The writer also obviously wants to omit punctuation in order to create opportunities to read some parts of the poem in more than one way.

Grammar:

The poem is one sentence, and is written in the form of a list of items, with descriptive terms attached to them. In some places, this directly imitates the structure of an 'Inventory', e.g. 'empty nutshells half filled' is like 'paint, two litres of' or 'lemons, fresh'.

In these cases, the modifiers would go after the nouns they modify – the opposite sequence to the norm for Standard English prose. The grammar is closely linked with the punctuation. The fact that there is no punctuation and the position of the line breaks mean that the modifiers could go either with the nouns before them or after them: for example, is it:

> 'empty nutshells half filled' or 'half filled ashtrays'?
> 'comb gap toothed' or 'gap toothed bookshelves'?

This helps to create a sense of uneasiness – the reader cannot pin down exactly which words should modify others; the writer wants to convey the uneasy, unsettled feeling that results from the departure of her lover.

Two parts of the poem could be read as sentences in their own right: 'you left me' and 'you shaped depression in my pillow' (if 'shaped' is taken as a verb). These depart from the idea of the list and make statements about the actions of the absent lover. They could be read as accusations.

Phonology:

There is extensive sound patterning in the poem via repetitions of various consonant groups and vowel sounds:

*n*othing	*n*ail			
*p*arings	*p*eel	*p*illow	sha*p*ed	de*p*ression
emp*ty*	*d*ir*ty*			
nut*shells*	book*shelves*			
a*sh*trays	*sh*aped	depre*ss*ion		
*l*eft	ha*lf*	*fil*led		
*c*ups	night*caps*	comb		

The sound patterning helps to give a sense of cohesion to the writing, making it seem tightly knit, by setting up echoes; at the same time, full rhyme is avoided, because that would seem too neat and would contradict with the impression the poem wants to give of loneliness and incompleteness and loss.

Semantics:

The nouns chosen move between domestic items and aspects of physical bodies; what links both groups of nouns is that they all relate to waste and after-effects created by human beings in their lives together: parings, peel, dregs, ash, hair, impressions on items from the weight of bodies. This suggests decay and the passage of time; domestic items still show where humans have been, even when the humans are long gone. A sense of sadness is therefore created. At one point, the connection between the human body and an inanimate object becomes metaphorical: the bookshelves have gaps in their teeth where the departing lover has taken his/her books away. The sense of emptiness is further underlined by the fact that there are many references to containers which are no longer full, items that have been spoiled or outsides of things which are no longer attached to their centres: parings, peel, empty nutshells, half filled ashtrays, dregs of nightcaps . . . The final 'you shaped depression' is the ultimate 'outside' of the departed lover, detached from the real person. The fact that the word 'depression' has been used both literally, to mean 'physical impression', and metaphorically, to mean 'feeling depressed', unites the two semantic strands of physical items and their psychological meaning, or connotations.

Discourse:

The writer has employed all the levels of language to convey a message on two levels: a simple list of items which have been left behind by a departing lover; the sadness felt by the speaker at the loss of that person. The use of particular line breaks and the lack of punctuation cut across the reader's ability to read the poem as a simple list; the fact that the reader is unsure how items and descriptions of them relate to each other creates a feeling of uneasiness and uncertainty, mirroring how the speaker feels, and the phonological patterning creates subtle echoes of sound which reinforce the idea of incompleteness; the choice of particular nouns which suggest the idea of containers, the idea of waste and decay, and the idea of inside/outside contrasts, all allow the poem to maintain the theme of physical and psychological loss.

Charity Appeal: Oxfam Advert

Graphology:

The advert has been constructed to look like someone has torn a section of writing from a book, and has ringed a part of it with his/her pen. This signals haste, urgency, concern, anger, the desire to take action – to show someone the extract, use it for some purpose. The same person has also written elsewhere on the text – underlining the word measles (presumably in shock that children in developing countries can still die of a disease that has long been curable in the West); stating that prevention is easy, and showing, via use of '. . .' that he/she is being reflective and thoughtful. The dots also move the reader on to focus on the inside page; endorsing Oxfam itself, in its efforts to prevent disease. The handwriting is capable, neat, well organised and confident.

The book from which the main extract has been torn is a textbook or reference book: this is suggested by the parts of words on either side of the main section – not in what the words might have said, but in the fact that this type of layout would be characteristic of a large reference book. There is a photograph of a very appealing healthy child – this fits with the overall message of preventive health care. The message is that you can prevent this child from becoming ill. The child is looking directly at the reader, and has its mouth open, as if it is communicating with the reader. The child could be either sex. The child's shoulders are visible, encouraging the reader to feel that he/she could touch and cuddle the child. 'Oxfam' is written boldly and straightforwardly, in upper case letters, and its symbol could suggest a child with its arms raised ready to be picked up, or a flower growing upright and strong. The essential message of the advert is written in bold upper case letters, in two parts – the main statement, which relates to the description on the torn-out text, and the addition following the dots, which pulls out the cause of disease and gives it extra prominence.

Phonology:

As this is a 'serious' text, little use is made of sound patterning. But there is some, to make the text memorable: fever/higher; vivid/florid; infected/inflamed; persistent and prolonged.

Semantics:

At first glance, the torn-out text appears to be from a medical textbook because of the many terms which refer to that area of knowledge; fever, appetite, rash, sores, coughing, diarrhoea, salts, nutrients. However, on closer inspection many dramatic and emotive terms and phrases are used which would not feature in this type of textbook: a vivid florid rash is appearing on the skin *as if from nowhere; open raw sores*; the diarrhoea is *unremitting*; water, salts and nutrients *are draining from the weakened body*; the thirst is *unbearable*; *racked by coughing fits*; the muscles of the *small heart*; *the lights of the body begin to go out*.

These uses of language trade on connotations rather than facts: the reader is having his/her emotions appealed to by language which highlights the tragedy of a young life being extinguished needlessly.

Grammar:

The text is written in the present tense, which would be characteristic of a textbook which describes symptoms of various diseases. But the text is also written as a dramatic story, and the present tense serves to reinforce the drama and tension. There are many uses of time adverbials: 'after a day or two'; 'as the days pass'; 'by the second week'; 'by now'. This provides a structure for the narrative.

The grammatical patterning includes many uses of listing involving repeats of similar structures: 'the fever is higher, appetite is gone, coughing begins'; 'the diarrhoea begins, the skin dries, and the rash spreads'; 'water, salts and nutrients'; 'infected and inflamed'; 'persistent and prolonged'. This technique, particularly when coupled with sound patterning, gives the text pace, force and memorability.

The final sentence of the passage has unusual word order, putting the main statement at the end in focus position to throw it into prominence: 'the lights of the body begin to go out'. The fact that this suggests the child's spirit, its essential life force, means that semantics and grammar are working together to create a climax. The technique of leaving the main part of the sentence to the end is an often used strategy to make the reader wait: this builds tension, while the reader is searching the passage to find the core of meaning. (In fact, the final sentence does not really make sense semantically, as it suggests that 'the lights of the body' are 'dehydrated', but the grammatical strategy still works.)

Discourse:

The text is trying to persuade the reader to act, and uses a number of strategies to that end, involving different language levels. It appears that someone has read the description of how children in developing countries still die in a gruesome way of measles, and they are angry and determined to take action. It is suggested that the real reader should do the same. The reader who has torn out the text endorses the work of Oxfam, and tells the real reader that taking action is easy and effective. The torn-out text, which looks like a medical description, is an emotive story which 'humanises' the medical facts and shows what happens to an individual child – like the healthy child in the photograph. It uses language which attempts to appeal to the reader's emotions by trying to convey what the child feels at each stage of the illness. The text is highly patterned grammatically, and builds to a climax which refers, not just to the child's body, but to something more intangible – its soul, spirit, or life force.

Genres Of Writing

'Genre' is a word of French origin, meaning 'type', or 'category'.

As a language user, you already know a great deal about different types or categories of writing. The work you have done in the previous section on different levels of language will help you in talking explicitly about written genres in the activities that follow.

INITIAL ACTIVITY: Genre Game

Below are some snippets from different written genres.

Decide which genre of writing each of the snippets has been taken from. Then use your own knowledge to make up ten more.

If you run out of ideas, think about some of the extracts you studied in the activities on language levels.

When you have finished your work in small groups, each group should circulate its sheet round the other groups, for them to guess.

If you have been working individually, test out your data on some informants, to see how far others are able to guess the genres.

SNIPPETS

1. In 1516, the Treaty was finally ratified by all parties . . .
2. A substance was placed over a bunsen burner and heated . . .
3. With Many Happy Returns . . .
4. In Loving Memory of . . .
5. She came to him in an agony of passion and tenderness . . .

When you have finished, consider the following:

● What were some of the clues you used to identify the snippets? Did these clues correspond with the language levels you studied previously?

● Which, if any, of the snippets were hard to guess, and why?

◆ ◆ ◆

FURTHER ACTIVITY: Dimensions of Written Variation

Now, using the headings below, fill in some details for the genres of writing you covered in the previous exercise.

Sometimes, the audience could be a number of different groups. In that case, it may be useful to fill in a range of possibilities.

| *Audience* | *Purpose* | *Format* |

If you have been working in groups, gather all your results together at the end on one large A3 sheet, and pin it up for everyone to see.

If you have been working individually, think carefully about the range of writing you have accounted for. As well as making you more aware of the range of written genres for the purposes of project research, your collation will help you to think about ideas for your original writing.

✦ ✦ ✦

Decoding Spoken Texts

Just as any reader knows a great deal about written texts and how they work, any speaker knows about spoken texts – their rules, as well as their features.

As speakers and listeners, we are not aware of all the different components which make up spoken communication; for example, in practice, we do not divorce intonation from vocabulary, or grammar from the physical gestures that we use.

However, for purposes of analysis, we need to break speech down into manageable elements, in order to see what part each of these elements plays in the whole act of communication. For this reason, this section is subdivided as follows:

1. It's The Way That You Say It
2. The Spoken Alphabet
3. The Speech Context
4. The Grammar of Speech
5. Spoken Vocabularies
6. The Rules of Interaction

Each subsection provides activities and speech extracts which illustrate the element being analysed; towards the end, you will have the chance to put these elements together, to see how they all work at once.

I. IT'S THE WAY THAT YOU SAY IT

Obviously, there is no such thing as punctuation in speech.

Written punctuation marks and other graphological devices are an attempt to suggest, for writing, what our voices do when we are talking.

INITIAL ACTIVITY I **or**

Read through the following examples and, paying particular attention to the punctuation in each, decide how the examples should be spoken when read aloud:

a) Hello. I said HELLO!
b) What on earth do you think you are doing?

c) She rose from her chair, walked to the door, and slammed it behind her.
d) No!!
e) It's pronounced 'hospital'.
f) Well, I don't know, really . . .
g) I didn't *mean* to do it – it just *happened*.
h) You can receive benefit (or the equivalent rebate) if you claim before the stated period.
i) He entered the room. The atmosphere was tense. Nobody spoke.
j) Take the following: a tablespoonful of grated Parmesan; three eggs, beaten lightly; a generous handful of basil, chopped coarsely; and a pinch of salt.

✦ ✦ ✦

If you were able to read the signals given by the punctuation marks and to turn them into vocal effects as you spoke, then you know a lot about the relationship between *written symbols* and *spoken intonation*.

When you want to transcribe a piece of real speech and represent in some detail how it actually sounded, however, written punctuation is a rather crude convention.

Real speech is not neat and tidy, like writing; it does not necessarily fit the written conventions of sentences (or even words, since we speak in bursts of sound); and written punctuation cannot do justice to the subtleties of intonation, pauses, and so on.

Transcription Conventions

Transcription conventions vary, but in many transcripts, boundary lines –/– are used to show pauses between utterances. Sometimes, transcribers also indicate longer pauses than average by using brackets, with a dot to represent a brief pause (but one which is longer than the 'norm' for a particular speaker) –(.)– and numbers of seconds for even longer pauses – (1), (2).

Pauses can be *filled* as well as silent, with speakers making noises such as 'er' or 'um' to keep their speech continuous.

INITIAL ACTIVITY II **or**

Read through the child's speech below, which has been marked with boundary lines. Read it aloud to hear how it sounded. Then decide:

— how the spoken divisions differ from the conventional sentence boundaries that you would have in writing;

— what the function is of the filled pauses.

er my name is Keir/and I'm six years old/and my best friend/is Matthew Harris/I go to Woodcote um/Woodcote Primary School/I think it's horrible/we're always doing work/my brother's um/three years old/and he's naughty/my worst enemy/is Darren Hunt/my second worst enemy/is David Harding/my third worst enemy/is Kalvin Racy

✦ ✦ ✦

Intonation

Intonation is a melody that we all sing.

If you compare speech with a song, then intonation is the backing tune to the words.

Intonation is our 'oral punctuation': our voices signal many meanings, including the message that one part of an utterance is ending and another is about to start. This ensures that the ambiguity which is often present on the page, in written material, is avoided in speech: for example, the sentence 'The terrorists wrecked the factory by blowing up the pipes' would never be ambiguous when spoken.

The divisions we make with intonation are called *tone groups*. These are the sections that you were looking at and reading aloud in the previous activity. Each tone group has one main stress, or intonation point. This is marked on the main stressed syllable in the group, which is called the *nuclear syllable*. Sometimes there is also a lighter stress before the main one, which is where the whole tune actually begins. This is called the *head*.

INITIAL ACTIVITY III

Read through the utterances below, and mark:

— where the main divisions (tone groups) would have been in each utterance;
— where the nuclear stress would have occurred for each tone group, with a * by the syllable;
— if there is a secondary, earlier stress before the main one (the head), with a '.

The first two examples have been completed, to start you off.

N.B. Assume that each utterance is conveying a straightforward, rather than any unusual, meaning. (Answers are on p.38.)

a) She'ran to the *station/and'caught the *train
b) He'fried the *onions/and'chopped the to*matoes
c) She went to London but wished she hadn't
d) They came in early and worked until lunchtime
e) He hurried along to the centre of town
f) I got a puncture while I was driving
g) After they left I was exhausted
h) She went to the bank at the end of the road
i) He hailed the bus and jumped on
j) Before I go I must make a phone call

Here is the transcript you worked on previously, with nuclear stress and heads marked. Try reading this aloud, interpreting the marked stresses and pauses:

er my'name is *Keir/and I'm'six years *old/and my'best *friend/is'Matthew *Harris/I'go to *Woodcote um//'Woodcote *Primary School/I'think it's *horrible/we're'always doing *work/'my *brother's um//'three years *old/and'he's *naughty/my'worst *enemy/is 'Darren *Hunt/'my *second worst enemy/is'David *Harding/'my *third worst enemy/is 'Kalvin *Racy

❖ ❖ ❖

Common Tone Groups

There are certain structures that often occur in tone groups, and there are examples of these in the data you have been studying.

Subject – Verb: My best friend/is Matthew Harris
                My worst enemy/is Darren Hunt

Co-ordination (linking with 'and'): They came in early/and worked until lunchtime
                                     My brother's three years old/and he's naughty

Subordination (linking with 'while 'after' 'when', etc.): I got a puncture/while I was driving; After they left/I was exhausted

Adverbials (words or phrases giving information about where, when or how actions were done): He hurried along/to the centre of town; She went to the bank/at the end of the road

Interjections and formulaic expressions: words and phrases like 'Well!' 'Now then!' 'Oh no!' 'Good morning!' often have their own tone groups. Sometimes this applies to fillers such as 'um' and 'er' as well.

Intonation Tunes

As well as placing a much heavier stress on the *nuclear syllable* in any tone group, we also sing a particular tune.

INITIAL ACTIVITY IV

To get some idea of the tunes we sing, have a conversation which involves no words, but try to get your meanings across to another person by using intonation alone.

Instead of speaking in words, use numbers – any will do, but two or three figure numbers will give you more of a chance to make your tune clear.

ANSWERS (INITIAL ACTIVITY III p.37)

a) She'ran to the *station/and'caught the *train
b) He'fried the *onions/and'chopped the to*matoes
c) She'went to *London/but'wished she *hadn't
d) They'came in *early/and'worked until *lunchtime
e) He'hurried a*long/to the'centre of *town
f) I'got a *puncture/'while I was *driving
g) 'After they *left//'I was ex*hausted
h) She'went to the *bank/at the'end of the *road
i) He'hailed the *bus/and'jumped *on
j) Be'fore I *go/I must'make a *phone call

Here are some of the meanings that you can try to convey to others:

anger	sympathy	sexiness
disagreement	reassurance	being impressed
sadness	joy	asking a question
issuing a command		

When you have finished your conversation, consider the following:

● How much meaning did you feel you could convey, using intonation alone?

FURTHER ACTIVITY I

We learn how to produce intonation tunes very early in life – when we are small babies. But there is a difference between being able to use intonation and being able to analyse it. The information that follows is all about the different intonation tunes that we use. Because the area is a complex one, and because it is being presented here on paper, you may well need to go over it several times. It is particularly important that you try out the various sounds as you go along.

There are seven main types of intonation *tune* in English, and each is marked in an individual way. There are also different types of *head*.

1. HIGH FALL: ˋAnn

This is where the voice starts high in pitch, and falls downwards.

It is very commonly used for straight statements, questions, and for commands, and, in these cases, takes a high head:

 I 'really ˋlike her
 I'm 'going on ˋTuesday
 'What are you ˋdoing?
 'How much is ˋthat?
 'Go aˋway!
 'Open the ˋdoor!

2. LOW FALL: ˏAnn

This is where the voice starts quite low in pitch, and falls downwards.

It is less commonly used than the high fall tune, but can be used to suggest the same sorts of meaning. However, low fall often conveys less enthusiasm and commitment because it sounds less energetic. Therefore it can mark weariness and irritation:

 What are you ˏdoing?
 Go aˏway!

3. HIGH RISE: ´Ann

This is where the voice starts high, and rises.

It can suggest shock and disbelief:

> What did you ´say?
> ´What?

It is also the tune that people often employ when they are calling up the stairs to someone who should have been downstairs long ago:

> ´John (Get up this minute, you're breakfast is getting cold!)

4. LOW RISE: ‚Ann

This is where the voice starts low, and rises.

It can create a caring and reassuring meaning, and, as such, is often used when adults speak to children (or animals!) in statement or question form. In these cases, it starts with a high head, so the beginning of the utterance is kept high:

> There's 'no need to ‚worry
> 'Did you have a nice ‚dinner?

When it is used with a low head, it can sound very grumpy:

> ‚You can't do ‚that

5. MID LEVEL: >Ann

This is the sound that we make when we want to imitate computerised or synthesized voices. It is right in the middle of our voice range, and to speak in it for any length of time makes us sound very robotic. It is the tune that teachers use when they are calling the register in a monotone:

> >Robert
> >Lisa
> >Janet
> >Peter

6. RISE-FALL: ^Ann

This is where the voice starts low, rises high, then falls again markedly in a short space of time. It is the sound we make when we are conveying a 'gossipy', 'well, you don't say', 'you are a naughty girl', 'ooh, I'm impressed' meaning:

> Get ^her/she got a dis^tinction

Frankie Howerd used this tune a lot: ^ah/^yes/^well/titter ye ^not/^no/^listen

It is also the sound that is used by other comedians to help create stereotypes of 'femaleness': for example, Les Dawson's gossipy older women, or John Inman's limp-wristed gay man in 'Are You Being Served?'.

7. Fall-Rise: ᵛAnn

This is the opposite of the above. The voice starts high, falls, then rises again in a short space of time.

This tune is used very frequently in English for a range of meanings. It is notoriously difficult for foreign learners to acquire, as it is not a straight movement of the voice, but a 'wobbly' sounding tune. It is most clearly expressed as a tune alone, with no accompanying words, by children when they are doing what we call 'whining'. Imagine a young child that you know has been told that he or she can't go to the park after all, because it's raining. The child utters a long-drawn out 'oh' sound with a whining intonation. This is an exaggerated fall-rise tune.

While in children's speech it often characterises disappointment, in adult dialogue it frequently expresses contrast, contradiction or warning, and, in these cases, is sometimes used with a falling head (ˋ):

> I ˋlike his ᵛwife (= but I don't like *him*)
> (He's thirty, isn't he?) ˋThirty ᵛfive
> (Dave couldn't make it) But ᵛPaul could
> You'll be ᵛlate

It can also be used for urging people on:

> Please ᵛtry

✦ ✦ ✦

FURTHER ACTIVITY II

Consider the following:

● What is the difference between these three ways of saying good morning?

> ′Good ˋmorning
> ′Good ˏmorning
> ′Good ˃morning

● Lists have a particular sequence of intonation tunes: all items until the last have a rising tune, then the final item on the list has a falling tune, to signal completion:

There's ˏwhisky/ ˏgin/ ˏbrandy/and ˋwine.

Now mark these slightly more complicated lists – from Margaret Thatcher's 1986 Education Speech, given to fellow Tories during the Conservative Party Conference. Listing (particularly in threes) is a persuasive device often used by public speakers. It is important that the speaker gets the intonation sequence right, or the public will be uncertain about when to clap.

Concentrate on the words in bold type, and mark in the boundaries and the tunes:

i) . . . to compete successfully in tomorrow's world **against Japan Germany and the United States**

ii) . . . we need **well educated well travelled creative young people**

● What is the difference in meaning between the falling and rising tunes in the following tag questions?

ᵗNice `day/`isn't it
ᵗThat's `right/ ‚isn't it

What would be the difference to the above if you reversed the intonation patterns, using rising tunes in the first, and falling in the second?

● The following conversation has the nuclear syllables marked in the wrong places, and the tunes marked are not necessarily the correct ones.

Read it aloud as it is written, to get a sense of why it is wrong.

Then write it out again, putting stresses in the right places, with the right tunes attached. The conversation is between two teachers, at exam time.

(Answers are on p.43.)

A: `what do I do/with these exam `papers
B: `sort them into bundles/`take them to the classrooms/and `dish them out
A: ^OK/`what else
B: `that's about it/`I think/how about `using your own initiative
A: `that's your job/I'm just a dogs`body

Speed and Volume

Musical tunes are not just about the notes being played. Factors such as the speed of the music, and the relative loudness of various parts of it, also play a part in how we interpret the melodies we hear.

The same is true of our voices. We vary the speed and volume of our speech to signal certain types of meaning, or as part of particular strategies in dialogue.

Transcribers sometimes use musical notation to describe speed and volume, as follows:

    Speed: allegro (fast)
            lente (slow)
            accelerando (accelerating)
            rallentando (slowing down)

    Volume: forte (loud)
            piano (soft)
            crescendo (becoming louder)
            diminuendo (becoming softer)

FURTHER ACTIVITY III or

Read through the conversation between Sir Robin Day and Margaret Thatcher, below.

Why do you think Margaret Thatcher starts her first utterance at high speed, then slows down to a more regular tempo?

Sir Robin Day: do you see a nation divided/between north and south/between the prosperous suburbs and the inner cities/between the employed and the unemployed/between the poverty stricken millions and the whizz kids of the big bang in the city

Margaret Thatcher: (allegro) I do not see a nation divided/in anything like the terms you say/(rallentando) or even divided in that way

Now look at the next conversation, which is between Jonathan Dimbleby and Margaret Thatcher. Why does Margaret Thatcher increase her volume at the beginning of her second turn, after Dimbleby's attempted interruption? (sections marked with asterisks *. . .* are spoken simultaneously by speakers)

Jonathan Dimbleby: do you believe/that as a result of this summit/we really are at the beginning of an new era/in east west relations/is it as important and dramatic/the process that is taking place in your view

Margaret Thatcher: I think the new era really began/when Mr Gorbachev made his famous speech/I think it was just the beginning of this year/making it quite clear/that the regime in the Soviet Union/wasn't producing the standard of living/the standard of technology/the standard of social services/all the hopes that people had had for it/over many years/and then that it had got to change/and then set out the kind of changes/more individual initiative/more personal responsibility/more personal involvement/this is very different/from the central planning *and control*

Jonathan Dimbleby: *do*/*do you*

Margaret Thatcher: (crescendo) *so that* was one thing/can I just say the other thing/is that he is the sort of person/who had both the vision to see this/and the courage and the boldness/to do something about it/and the other thing/he is a quite different soviet leader/from any other I have met/his discussion ranges widely/over any subject/ normally they read from a rather sterile brief/not so Mr Gorbachev/so yes/that did offer the hope of a new age

◆ ◆ ◆

---

2. THE SPOKEN ALPHABET

You have seen in the previous section that written punctuation cannot represent the many subtle meanings conveyed by intonation.

In the same way, the written alphabet cannot represent the many different ways in which one word could be pronounced by people from different parts of the country – in other words, *accent features*.

In the real speech context, speakers are very skilled at registering and interpreting accent variations – both the way in which speakers from different areas differ from each other, and the way in which one speaker can vary his or her accent during the course of a conversation, to signal certain meanings.

Because writing is a standardised medium (i.e. everyone learns and uses the same system), it does not easily represent such subtle differences.

The *phonemic alphabet* is a way of transcribing the actual sounds that people make. A *phoneme* is 'a single, distinctive sound'. The phonemic alphabet is better than the spelling alphabet for describing sounds because one spelling can have different sounds – cough, through – and one sound have different spellings – meat, feet.

The phonemic alphabet on p.45 is based on the RP – Received Pronunciation – accent (the accent generally used by national newsreaders).

INITIAL ACTIVITY I

One person should read out the words from the list below and the other member of the pair should write them down as they were actually said. If you want to share the speaking and transcribing tasks, split the list in half, and each read 14 words.

If you are working individually, ask someone to read the words aloud to you.

The person reading the words should try to reproduce them in as natural a way as possible, and not try to use a more formal pronunciation than is usual. He/she may have to say the words several times in order for the transcriber to keep up. The transcriber needs to forget about the spelling of the words, and listen very carefully to the sounds that are actually being made.

WORD LIST

THERE	CITY	PUTT	THREE
BUS	AFTER	PULL	OFF
CAR	FUR	POOL	BOTTLE
BATH	FAIR	POOR	HOSPITAL
DOWN	WHO	FAR	ROAD
COT	HUGH	FIRE	ABOUT
DANCE	PUT	SINGING	THEM

✦ ✦ ✦

THE ENGLISH PHONEMIC ALPHABET (Based on the RP accent)

LIST OF SYMBOLS

	English Vowels			English Consonants	
1.	i	as in s<u>ee</u>	1.	p	as in <u>p</u>ut
2.	ɪ	as in s<u>i</u>t	2.	b	as in <u>b</u>ut
3.	e	as in s<u>e</u>t	3.	t	as in <u>t</u>en
4.	æ	as in s<u>a</u>t	4.	d	as in <u>d</u>en
5.	a	as in c<u>a</u>lm	5.	k	as in <u>c</u>ome
6.	ɒ	as in n<u>o</u>t	6.	g	as in <u>g</u>o
7.	ɔ	as in b<u>ou</u>ght	7.	tʃ	as in <u>ch</u>ur<u>ch</u>
8.	ʊ	as in p<u>u</u>t	8.	dʒ	as in <u>j</u>u<u>dge</u>
9.	u	as in b<u>oo</u>t	9.	m	as in <u>m</u>ake
10.	ʌ	as in c<u>u</u>p*	10.	n	as in <u>n</u>et
11.	ɜ	as in b<u>ir</u>d	11.	ŋ	as in lo<u>ng</u>
12.	ə	as in <u>a</u>bout	12.	l	as in <u>l</u>ong
13.	eɪ	as in pl<u>ay</u>	13.	f	as in <u>f</u>ull
14.	əʊ	as in g<u>o</u>	14.	v	as in <u>v</u>ery
15.	aɪ	as in m<u>y</u>	15.	θ	as in <u>th</u>in
16.	aʊ	as in n<u>ow</u>	16.	ð	as in <u>th</u>en
17.	ɔɪ	as in c<u>oi</u>l	17.	s	as in <u>s</u>at
18.	ɪə	as in h<u>ere</u>	18.	z	as in <u>z</u>eal
19.	ɛə	as in th<u>ere</u>	19.	ʃ	as in <u>sh</u>ip
20.	ʊə	as in cr<u>ue</u>l	20.	ʒ	as in mea<u>s</u>ure
			21.	r	as in <u>r</u>un
			22.	h	as in <u>h</u>at
			23.	w	as in <u>w</u>ent
			24.	j	as in <u>y</u>et

*the RP pronunciation of 'cup'.

Many northern speakers do not have this phoneme in their speech.

There is one more sound which is often used, but is not listed above because it is not a full sound. This is the *glottal stop,* and is written as ?. It is similar to the 'h' sound, but differs from it by being produced by closing the vocal cords, as you would when you pick up a heavy weight. It sometimes replaces other sounds in certain accents, for example, Cockney speakers would say bɒʔəl

compared with RP bɒtəl

INITIAL ACTIVITY II 👤 or ⬤

Now compare your results with the RP accented versions of the words, given below:

● Which major differences in sound characterise the speech of your region?

● Are you aware of different ways of pronouncing some of the words on the word list, even though they may not be the pronunciations you yourself use?

WORD LIST

	RP pronunciation	*Notes on other accents*
THERE	ðɛə	Liverpool = ð3 ; Patwa = dɛə
BUS	bʌs	Northern = bʊs
CAR	ka	West Country = kar
BATH	baθ	Northern = bæθ
DOWN	daʊn	Irish = dəʊn
COT	kɒt	Scottish = kɔt
DANCE	dans	Northern = dæns
CITY	sɪtɪ	North East = sɪti
AFTER	aftə	Salford (Manchester) = æftɒ
FUR	f3	} Liverpool — both = f3
FAIR	fɛə	
WHO	hu	} Norfolk — both = hu
HUGH	hju	
PUT	pʊt	} Northern — both = pʊt
PUTT	pʌt	
PULL	pʊl	Irish = pul
POOL	pul	Liverpool = puːl *
POOR	pɔ	Scottish = pʊə
FAR	fa	} Advanced RP** — both = fa
FIRE	faɪə	
SINGING	sɪŋɪŋ	Many regional accents = sɪŋɪn
THREE	θri	Cockney = fri ; Patwa = tri
OFF	ɒf	Advanced RP = ɔf
BOTTLE	bɒtəl	Cockney = bɒʔəl
HOSPITAL	hɒspɪtəl	Cockney = ʔɒspɪʔəl
ROAD	rəʊd	Lancs/Yorks = rɔd ; Liverpool = rəʊːd
ABOUT	əbaʊt	Cockney = əbaʊt
THEM	ðem	Cockney = vem ; Patwa = dem

* : indicates that the vowel sound is held for longer than in RP.
** 'Advanced RP' refers to the way RP used to sound years ago. This accent is now used only by relatively few speakers.

◆ ◆ ◆

FURTHER ACTIVITY

The work that you have done on sounds so far has related to regional accent features, and has involved speakers reading items on a word list aloud. When people read isolated words aloud, they are usually very careful about their pronunciation, and the way they speak will differ from how they would be in informal conversation.

There are certain aspects of spoken language which come into play when we say words in a piece of connected speech, and these aspects are present whatever accent we happen to have. This activity will help you to understand these aspects of connected speech.

One person in each group should read the passage below onto a tape. The reader should try to read in as relaxed a manner as possible.

Then each group should transcribe the sounds made by the reader, using the phonemic alphabet. Work together on this, helping each other to decide exactly what sounds were made.

If you are working individually, ask someone to read the passage for you onto a tape.

PASSAGE

She found her handbag and pulled out a white handkerchief. Her secretary, Peter Andy, had made her a celebration meal in honour of the good news: a platter of cold meats, hot-pot, followed by tinned peaches and cream, and about ten cups of coffee to sober them up after the champagne.

Her handbag gaped too wide for me to ignore the object which met my open, two-eyed gaze: a box from India or China, with delicate carvings and the initials 'E.E.N.'.

When you have transcribed the passage, look particularly at the following aspects of connected speech:

Assimilation

This is where a sound changes under the influence of another.

For example, how was 'ten cups' pronounced by the reader? Was it the following:

$$teŋ \; kʌps \; ?$$

If so, this is assimilation, as n becomes ŋ so that the mouth is in the right position to say the k in 'cups'.

Make a list of any other examples of assimilation you can find.

You might check how the following were said:

handbag   handkerchief   good news   tinned peaches

ɦæŋkətʃif   gʊbnjʊz   tɪmpitʃɪz

Elision

This is where a sound is left out from a word, when it would normally be pronounced if the word was said in isolation.

For example, how was 'secretary' pronounced by the reader? Was it the following:

sekrətri ?

If so, this is elision, as when the word is pronounced in isolation, people will normally say:

sekrətari

Make a list of any other examples of elision you can find.

You might check how the following were said, paying attention to whether the sounds in bold type were actually pronounced:

col**d** meats   hot-pot   **h**andbag   **h**andkerchief   **h**er   matter of

Liaison

This is where linking sounds are inserted by speakers, so that there is a smooth transition from one word to another. The sounds that are inserted are often r, j or w.

For example, was 'two-eyed' pronounced as: tʊ w̲aɪd ?

If so, this is an example of liaison, because the w sound was inserted as a linking device.

Make a list of any other examples of liaison you can find. You might check how the following were said, paying attention to whether any linking sounds were added that would not have been present if the words were said in isolation:

my open   India or China

maɪ j̲əʊpən   ɪndiər̲ ɔ tʃaɪnə

Juncture

This is where speakers make a special effort to keep words distinct from each other.

This often involves the use of the glottal stop – not to replace sounds, but to separate them. For example, did your reader say: pitarændi or pita?ændi ?

If it was the second alternative, this is juncture, as the glottal stop is being used to create a boundary. Why should the reader want to create a boundary between these two words? If your reader said the first alternative, this is an example of elision. Your reader obviously saw no need to keep the words separate.

Make a list of any more examples of juncture that you can find. You might check how your reader said the following: E.E.N.

Check your transcriptions against the notes above.

(There may well be variations according to the different readings you were transcribing.)

Has this activity helped you to understand how connected speech can differ from words pronounced in isolation?

The aspects of connected speech you have been studying are present in the spoken language of everyone, whatever their accent may be, and become more noticeable as speakers relax and sound less formal.

Were the readers of the passage conscious of trying to be careful in their speech?

How could you collect speech that was less self-conscious than the reading of the passage?

❖ ❖ ❖

3. THE SPEECH CONTEXT

Speech differs from writing in being supported by the physical setting in which it takes place. Physical gestures, for example, often have a meaning in their own right (think of the behaviour of drivers in traffic jams, or the many gestures that are used in sign language by deaf speakers). Many physical gestures are also language specific: for example, a 'thumbs up' sign, which is innocent and positive for English speakers, is very rude in Spanish.

The physical setting has an effect on the language that is used in spoken communication. For example, the fact that speakers can see objects that are being referred to means that the full names of the objects don't have to be used. Words like 'these, those, this, that' are often all that are needed: these are called *deictics*, which means 'pointing words'. The fact that speakers register each others' meanings and feelings as speech takes place means that language doesn't always need to be fully explicit: much can be left out. For example, a speaker recalling an upsetting experience might say '. . . and then I felt, you know . . .' The listener would fill in the details not fully explained. This missing out of details that are understood is called *ellipsis*.

INITIAL ACTIVITY I

Look at the extract below. What activity do you think the speakers are engaged in?

A: if you start here/um/what you can do/is take this up gradually/stopping to just check/this is even/*then*
B: *what* about this side/how do you keep it/out of the way
A: well/just get one of these/and clip it up/and forget about it
B: right/so take that up *gradually*
A: *yeah*/and make sure it's level/don't get carried away/you can always come back to it later
B: so then which way do you go
A: up here/then the same the other side/the top and front last/then you can see for yourself/how the shape's coming on/and the top and front/should take their shape/from the rest/that's the skill really/judging as you go/even though you have the main idea/in your head

(Answer on p.51.)

Consider the following:

● What clues did you get about the activity the speakers were engaged in, to help you understand all the references to 'here', 'there', 'this' and so on?

◆ ◆ ◆

INITIAL ACTIVITY II

Write a short conversation between two or more speakers who are engaged in a particular activity.

Imagine that the speakers are talking as they are working, referring to what they are doing. Try not to give the answer away too easily: use examples of deictics and ellipsis.

When you have finished, read your conversation aloud to the other groups, for them to guess what your speakers were doing. If the other groups cannot guess, act out your conversation with the appropriate physical gestures.

If you are working individually, read your conversation aloud to someone, and ask him/her to guess the activity.

◆ ◆ ◆

4. THE GRAMMAR OF SPEECH

Speech is just as structured as writing, but its 'rules' are sometimes different.

As speakers, we have to hold quite a lot of information in our minds while we talk, so we don't mind repetition. Giving more information than is strictly necessary is sometimes referred to as *redundancy*. For the same reason – the need to process information as we talk – we often prefer structures that are easy to unravel, for example, the use of 'and' as a connective, rather than more complex connectives such as 'while' or 'since'.

In writing, we try to avoid redundancy; we also try to vary the connectives that we use, so that, while 'and' is the norm in speech, in writing it is used only sparingly.

As speakers, we are also aware of the spontaneous nature or *immediacy* of speech, so we accept, and even expect, many structures that would be thought of as untidy or wrong in writing because we know that writers have plenty of time to edit and revise their language. For example, in speech we have false starts, complete changes of direction in mid-utterance, and utterances trailing off or not fitting together structurally, even though they make complete sense to the people in the conversation. David Crystal calls slips of the tongue, hesitations, back-tracking, and other features that result from the 'here and now' nature of speech as *normal non-fluency features*, and says that we are suspicious of speakers who do not use them – we rate such people as rather unnatural – too well-rehearsed to be genuine.

Speakers also use *fillers* to give themselves thinking time; *initiators* like 'well' or 'OK, then' or 'right' at the beginning of their utterances, to signal the fact that they are about to speak; and *vague completers* such as 'and that' or 'and everything' to round off what they have said. These structures are devices which help speakers give shape to their utterances.

None of these features would be considered appropriate in writing, unless we were writing a piece of dialogue that was trying to imitate real speech.

Another difference in the 'rules' we apply to speech and writing is that writing is expected to conform more to *Standard English*, while speech, especially in informal contexts, is allowed more *regional dialects*. This includes grammar, as well as vocabulary; so phrases like 'I ain't done nothing' and 'we was' are tolerated much more in speech than in writing.

A major difference between the nature of speech and writing is that speech is *interactive*. Many informal conversations involve fast exchanges between participants; but even where one speaker is holding the floor for some time, there is still an awareness of audience which affects the language structures used. For example, listeners are expected to offer *reinforcements* such as 'mm' and 'yeah', to reassure the speaker that what is being said is valuable; speakers often use *monitoring* features, such as 'you know?' and 'do you know what I mean?', to check that what they are saying is being attended to. Writing does not have this intimate give-and-take: even the fastest form of written exchange – the fax – is still very slow in comparison.

The grammar of speech is also coloured by what we are using speech for at any particular time, and specific kinds of interactions will contain certain types of grammatical structures: for example, teaching situations are likely to contain many examples of questioning; children at play may well be trying to direct each other's behaviour, in which case they will be using commands; jokes and stories have their own particular shape that speakers stick to as part of the genre. The differences between different types or *genres* of speech will be explored later.

ANSWER (INITIAL ACTIVITY I p.50)

Hairdressing

INITIAL ACTIVITY I

Read through the conversation below and:

— identify some of the structures in the data that are characteristic of speech;

— discuss the different types of questions used by the interviewer. Why does the first question elicit a very short response, while the second stimulates a much longer answer?

(Notes on this activity are on p.53.)

A = an 'A' Level student; B = a primary school pupil

A: what we want to do/is ask you some questions/about things that you've written/you wrote about um a space story/didn't you

B: yeah

A: what was that about

B: well um/we were doing about space/so I wrote a story about um/me and my friend/went up to space/and we um/and we saw um this alien/with um six eyes/and two mouths/and one nose/and um then/we um picked up some stones/to take back to England/and we um/we um drove out out in/we went out into space/and um we looked/and we and we didn't want/to go back to England/but um we stayed up there/for six days/then we all flew back to England/and then we showed the um rock/that we brought back.

✦ ✦ ✦

INITIAL ACTIVITY II

Read through the material below, which is the transcribed speech of a 79 year-old Lincolnshire speaker. Pick out:

— any structures which you consider to be examples of regional dialect grammar;

— any structures which you consider to be typical of informal speech in general (but not dialect).

Make two lists for the features above. When you have finished, consider how far any of the structures you have picked out could be used in Standard English *writing*.

(Notes on this activity are on p.53.)

SPEECH

well/I'm Harry Bruntlett/I live at number one Mill Lane/Louth/my age is seventy-nine year old/now when I started school/I was at Withcall/in those days/and we had to go right through them cuttings/they was all chalk/you used to go with your shoes clen/in a morning/and you got there/you thought you'd a pair of cricket sandals on/by golly/it was a mess/now where did we go then/we went/we left there/and we went to Kelstern/and I used to go to the shop there/and fetch a loaf of bread for tuppence/and a bottle of pop/it was tuppence/and the big bottles was fourpence/and they had them glass alleys in them days/you had to put a stopper in/and give it a thump/and you wanted to get the bottle/to your mouth/or you'd lost half on it in gas/it had just gone all up/aye/and what else was it/where did we go there/from Kelstern/on we went to Lanscroft/now I had to go to work/when I was twelve/on a Saturday/and (laughter) you didn't get a deal for it/neither/I'll tell you/aye/twelve on a Saturday/it was/and I left school/when I was fourteen/and I had to go to service/and I got to see to four horses/and I got fourteen pounds a year/my overtime on harvest time/was fourpence/and I/of course we come to Keddington then/and er/so then we was in the Louth area then/we'd a gas house in them days/we used to be leading coal/and making the gas like/you could get a bag of coal for four/for er two shillings/so it was/and Jacksons/they had no end of lorries of coal/in the coalyard like/leading lorries of coal out/and there was Wilemans/and no end on them/but by golly/things is altered/I can remember them building Lacey Gardens/them houses at Lacey Gardens/I was a boy/when it used to be a road/I can remember the men building that/aye/I don't know

---

Notes (Initial Activity I p.52)

Features characteristic of speech
    Initiator: well
    Filler: um
    Connectives: frequent use of 'and'
    Repetitions: drove out out; and we and we
    Change of course: out out in/we went out
    Utterances not fitting together structurally: so I wrote a story about um/me and my friend went up to space
    Particular use of 'this' for indefinite reference: this alien

Questioning
    The first question is a closed question: only certain responses are possible. In fact, because this particular question is a positive statement with a negative tag, the response 'yes' is strongly conditioned. Compare this with: It's a nice day, isn't it? It's rotten weather, isn't it? They're great shoes, aren't they?
    The second question is much more open, inviting the child to give a recount of the story, which invitation he takes up.

Notes (Initial Activity II p.52)

Regional Dialect Grammar
    Demonstrative 'them': them cuttings; them glass alleys; them days; them houses
    Prepositions: in a morning; half on it; on a Saturday; on harvest time; no end on them
    Verb 'to be': they was all chalk; the big bottles was fourpence; we was in the Louth area; things is altered
    Present form of the verb used for past tense meaning: we come to Keddington
    Singular noun for plural: seventy-nine year old
    Contractions: we'd; you'd (for we had/you had rather than we would/you would)
    Negatives: I didn't get a deal for it neither
    Other phrases: what else was it; so it was
    Dialect vocabulary: aye; clen; a deal; alleys

Informal Speech
    well; now; like (meaning 'as it were'); by golly; bottle of pop; I'll tell you; I don't know; to see to four horses; no end of lorries

5. SPOKEN VOCABULARIES

All speakers have a range or *repertoire* of different styles of speech from which they select in specific situations. For monolingual speakers, these different styles will involve changes in accent, grammar and vocabulary within the same language; for bilingual or multilingual speakers, the variations may well involve *mixing* aspects of their different languages together, or *switching* completely from one language to another for a considerable period of time.

Regardless of the number of languages speakers have in their repertoires, their choices of style – and therefore vocabulary, as an important ingredient of style – will be highly dependent on a number of factors. Some of these are the following:

Status – The status of the person you are talking to will have an influence on how formal a style you choose. For example, if you are talking to a person who is higher status than yourself, you are likely to become more formal. In this situation, your vocabulary is unlikely to include such items as slang terms, intimate forms of address, swear words, and vague expressions such as 'thingy' or 'whatsit'.

The number of people you are addressing will also be influential: in general, people become more formal as they address bigger groups.

Setting – A formal setting, such as an interview, will trigger more carefully chosen and formal vocabulary than, say, an informal chat with friends on a bus or in the pub.

Purpose – What you are using your language for will influence your vocabulary: if you are telling a humorous anecdote, for example, your vocabulary may well differ from that you would use in a serious debate or when giving a set of instructions.

Topic – Some topics are likely to make speakers more careful in their choice of words. We are particularly careful when we refer to taboo areas like death, sex, or bodily functions – although this doesn't necessarily mean that we become more formal. We may go the other way, and select terms that are considered 'impolite'. The fact that we may go to extremes in this way is an indication that the subject matter is uncomfortable or embarrassing to us.

Channel – The choice of channel, or medium – speech itself, as opposed to writing – is also likely to influence the style we use. Writing is, in general, a more formal channel than speech, if, as our definition of speech, we have 'informal conversation between friends in a relaxed setting'. Our most common interactions – spontaneous exchanges with partners, relatives, friends and acquaintances about the facts and experiences of day-to-day living – do not involve us in using a particularly formal style or wide-ranging vocabulary. However, it is dangerous to draw up generalisations which try to cover all forms of speech or writing, as there are many different types of each.

INITIAL ACTIVITY

The aim of this activity is to explore and compare two very different spoken interactions. Read them through, then compare them in terms of formality of style. Decide which is the more formal of the two, and consider which of the triggering factors you have been reading about has been influential in the two dialogues. Look particularly carefully at the choice of vocabulary and make a list of examples of formal/informal terms.

Also consider any of the other aspects of speech you have been working on during this section. When you have finished, make some notes on your discussions ready to feed back to the whole group, if you have been working in a class situation. If you have been working individually, write down some notes for your own use.

DIALOGUE 1

This is a conversation between two 16 year-old students on the way home on the bus. They are discussing the forthcoming prize-giving event at their school. *. . .* = overlapping speech.

A: got a prize
B: GCSEs
A: oh yeah
B: as has most of the world
A: well
B: as you go up to the top/stand with your top two feet together/on the top step/so you don't fall/get hold of his hand/thank you very much/Professor Ashworth/now it's got/it's not just you say it once/but you've got well three years/hundred in each year/three hundred *girls*
A: *yeah*
B: quite a lot are getting two prizes/or something/so you sort of probably got five hundred kids/walking up to him/saying thank you very much Mist/I mean he'll get bloody bored/isn't he
A: (laughter)
B: standing there/just shaking all these hands/saying/having all these kids saying/thank you very much Mist/Professor Ashworth/I wouldn't mind/but no one can say it/Profesher Affworth
A: (laughter) and spit at him

DIALOGUE 2

This is an extract from a televised interview between Sir Robin Day and Margaret Thatcher.

Sir Robin Day: are wages here/running too high

Margaret Thatcher: wages here/yes/are still running too high/in proportion to what we produce/although the er CBI did say er/and I think/they have some reason to say it/that unit wage costs/are not rising now/as fast as our competitors/you know/what that means/is that at last/the fantastic investment they have put in/is increasing productivity/it means of course/that we still have a problem/with unemployment/but the CBI did say recently/and it is good news/as far as competing is concerned/that our unit wage costs/are rising more slowly/but there is there/we have had one thing/in this country/that others didn't have/you know/during the period of prices and incomes policy/people got used almost as a right/to an annual increase/regardless of whether it has been earned/and we are still suffering from that/because really/you ought to have to earn your increase/if they/if you are to keep the value of your money/absolutely steady

❖ ❖ ❖

FURTHER ACTIVITY

Consider in some detail how the two dialogues in the previous activity differ in formality, in particular:

— how do the two conversations differ in the triggering factors that are influencing their style (status, setting, purpose, topic)?

— highlight some examples of the differences in vocabulary you listed;

— what other aspects of spoken language are important differences between the two dialogues?

If you have been working individually, write up your notes in summary, essay form.

6. THE RULES OF INTERACTION

Some aspects of speech which result from its interactive nature have already been suggested in this section: for example, the way intonation is used to signal the end of a speaker's turn (or the wish to continue); the use of deictics and ellipsis, reflecting the shared speech context; the use of particular structures connected with the need for speakers and listeners to register each others' reactions; the use of questioning as an interactive strategy; vocabulary and language choice which reflects the relationship between the participants, their shared setting, purpose, topic and channel. This last section aims to look particularly at how speakers and listeners organise turn-taking, and at some very general rules which exist in our minds about how conversations should be conducted.

The Etiquette of Conversation

A linguist, H. P. Grice, tried to set out in very simple terms some of the 'rules' we take for granted in our interactions.

He said that conversation is a co-operative activity, where speakers work together for an agreed purpose, each person trying to help shape the conversation with his or her contribution. So one basic rule is that speakers are trying to be *helpful and co-operative*.

Here are some of the rules or *conversational maxims* which speakers try to follow:

1. Maxim of Quantity

Give as much information as is required, but not more than is required.

This is saying that we try to be as explicit and specific as possible.

2. Maxim of Quality

a) Do not say what you believe to be false.

b) Do not say that for which you lack adequate evidence.

This is saying that we try to tell the truth, and that we feel we should have some reasons for our opinions.

3. *Maxim of Relation*

Be relevant.

This says that we try to stick to the point.

4. *Maxim of Manner*

a) Avoid obscurity.
b) Avoid ambiguity.
c) Avoid unnecessary wordiness.
d) Be orderly.

These points relate to the way we talk – in other words, to our style. They suggest that we try to make our contributions clear, concise and well organised.

General

Grice claims that, in general, we aim for *economy* but *clarity*, so that we don't constantly have to stop the conversation to ask people what they meant.

If we are unclear about meaning, we go through the following procedure:

● We search the preceding conversation for some kind of connection

● If that fails, we search the physical context we are in

● If that fails, we go to our long-term memories

● If that fails, we ask!

Because we have a rule that conversations are co-operative forms of behaviour, we make lots of assumptions and 'read between the lines' when people speak. For example, in the following conversation:

A: I've run out of petrol. Is there a garage around here?
B: There's one up the road.

A assumes that B is indicating the garage up the road sells petrol, and is open.

Similarly, in the following exchange, A assumes B believes the corkscrew will be in one or other of the places mentioned:

A: Where's the corkscrew?
B: Try the drawer or the cupboard.

Grice calls this 'reading between the lines' conversational implicature.

INITIAL ACTIVITY I  or

Look at the descriptions of faults in the way people talk below. Try to match them to the maxims you have just been reading about: what rules are these people breaking?

a bore	a scatterbrain	a liar
a stirrer	a shifty person	a con-man
a gossip	a wind-bag	withdrawn
vague	elliptical	abstruse

Consider the following questions:

● Can you add to this list?

● Can you think of any people you know, who have the conversational faults above?

● Do you agree with Grice that we do have 'rules' for how we behave in conversations?

● Would you add any further rules of your own, to describe our behaviour in interactions?

◆ ◆ ◆

Some More Rules

1. *Turn-taking*

Turn-taking is an important aspect of the way speakers co-operate in conversations.

The basic rule of taking turns ensures that one speaker talks at a time, and that a change of speaker occurs.

The process of turn-taking involves active listenership as well as speakership. While speakers ask their listeners monitoring questions – such as 'do you know what I mean?' (see *The Grammar of Speech* p.50) listeners give speakers a variety of signals about how the talk is being received. Reinforcements ('mm', 'yeah') given by listeners at regular intervals encourage speakers to continue; however, if reinforcements come too frequently, with a mid-level intonation, or if they come too infrequently, speakers become discouraged, and eventually dry up. Telephone conversations involve speakers and listeners in being particularly attentive to such signals, since other supports are absent. In face-to-face conversation, non-verbal behaviour (i.e. body language) plays a large part in turn-taking: for example, as speakers are drawing to a close in their turn, they often look directly at the person they are going to hand over to; at the same time, if listeners want to get a turn, they look directly at the speaker in order to signal this.

2. *Interruptions*

Listeners' reinforcements can take the form of enthusiastic overlaps, or longer utterances which interrupt the speaker completely for a while. Speakers know the difference between the kinds of intrusions which are the result of listeners' enthusiasm and other types of interruption which are attempts by listeners to take over the conversation and have a turn. Listeners may use their turn to offer a new perspective on the existing topic, or by starting a new topic altogether.

3. *Topic Changes*

Speakers engaged in conversation can range over many topics in a very short space of time. We do not require strong links between topics in speech – unlike writing, where ideas are often arranged thematically, in paragraphs, and readers expect paragraphs to be clearly linked. Topics may change as new speakers take over; but existing speakers can also move through a number of topics within one turn. Often, a speaker who is trying to get a listener to talk will try many different topics in order to find one that the listener will be able to take up.

INITIAL ACTIVITY II 👤 or 👤👤👤

Read through the conversation below, and try to make some sense of what was going on. The dialogue took place in a queue in a sandwich shop near to a sixth form college in Manchester.

The speakers are all students who know each other very well.

E = Emma   K = Kate   P = Philip   N = Nicola
. . . = overlapping speech

E: listen/right/I went to the toilet/and we went near this sand pit/right/and I got up the next morning/and all my shoes/were caked in white stuff/cement/or summat/oh god/what's it been like at college then/alright/I'm knackered/me/I'm dead tired/I can't stand this weather/it's too warm/*I*
K: *where's* Stephanie today
E: she'll be here/in a bit/we've got a lesson/I think/I hope she's got a lesson/anyway
P: (laughter) I had ice-cream/on there/(indicates record album he is holding) so I licked it off/because it was on *Madonna*
E: *wooh*/Philip
K: where did you go/this weekend
E: number one/on Friday night
K: we went on Saturday
E: I didn't see anyone I knew/on Friday night
K: no/most of them go/on Saturdays
E: I went in/and the bouncer/was all over me/wasn't he *Phil*
P: *mmm*/that bouncer/was well after *her*
E: *and* he went/and he/eh/we nearly got fuckin' chucked out/of this other club/'cause of you
N: *me*
E: *yeah*/callin' *everyone*
P: *(laughter)*
E: Stephs at it/I'm gonna kill Nicky

Now consider and make notes on the following questions, either in preparation for feedback to the whole group, or for your own individual file:

● Consider the various speakers' contributions in the light of Grice's 'conversational maxims'. Do any of the speakers break the rules, and, if so, how?

- How does the turn-taking procedure work in the conversation?

- Which of the examples of overlapping speech are reinforcements for the speaker to continue, and which are attempts to interrupt in order to get a turn?

- How many topics are attempted during the course of the conversation? How are changes of topic achieved?

- Consider some of the other areas of spoken language you have studied in this section. For example, what part is played in the conversation by such aspects as: the speech context and non-verbal behaviour; deictics and ellipsis; use of regional dialect vocabulary and grammar; normal non-fluency features? What comments would you make about the vocabulary used in the dialogue? What triggering factors have influenced the participants' choice of language?

Genres Of Speech

Just as we use written language for a variety of purposes, so we have a range of spoken genres which are used in different situations for particular reasons.

This section aims to explore what speakers know about varieties of spoken text, and what their characteristics are.

INITIAL ACTIVITY

Read through the pieces of spoken language below, and, for each, decide:

a) where the utterance has been taken from, i.e. what genre of speech it represents;
b) how you knew the answer to point a) above: what aspects of the language made it typical of a particular genre?

SPOKEN LANGUAGE

1. I name this ship . . .
2. We are gathered here today to celebrate the union of . . .
3. Lords, Ladies and Gentlemen . . .
4. You have the right to remain silent, but anything you say . . .
5. Have you heard the one about . . .
6. Right, settle down now, today we're going to look at . . .
7. I'm afraid I can't take your call at the moment, but if you'd like to leave me a message . . .
8. Good morning, the St. Clair Foundation, Diana speaking, can I help you? . . .
9. Hello, are you looking for anything particular, Madam? . . .
10. One potato, two potato, three potato, four . . .

11. Listen, this really weird thing happened to me last week . . .
12. Hi, Phil Drew here, taking you through all the way to midday . . .
13. Hello, this is Janet here, calling at 11.15 on Tuesday . . .
14. Dave, this is Mike from work. Mike, this is my partner, Dave . . .
15. Madam Speaker, I should like to ask my honourable friend whether he . . .
16. Space, the final frontier. This the voyage of . . .
17. Eyes down looking for a full house . . .
18. Tinker, tailor, soldier, sailor, rich man . . .
19. Can't beat the real thing . . . can't beat the feeling!
20. We apologise for the late arrival of the 9.15 from Crewe . . .

Were you surprised at:

— how quickly you were able to categorise the extracts above?
— how many different genres of speech there must be in use in society?
— how many spoken 'rituals' we have? (e.g. certain set phrases and formulas that we expect in particular situations). Can you think of any more spoken rituals? Here are some ideas to get you started:

What do you say in the following situations:

● When you want to end a conversation on the phone?

● When you pick the phone up?

● When you want to get off the bus, and you need someone to let you out from your seat?

● When you walk into a restaurant where you booked a table for dinner?

◆ ◆ ◆

FURTHER ACTIVITY I

Look again at the extracts from different genres on p.60.

Different spoken genres are sometimes called *speech events*: a speech event is a whole interaction with a specific purpose. Even a casual exchange of words at the bus stop with a stranger has a purpose: that of acknowledging that you are two people in a common situation, two human beings who are prepared to be friendly. The purely social, 'human contact' purpose of some of our interactions, where the contact itself is more important than the words, is often called *phatic communion*. This phrase was invented by an anthropologist called Bronislaw Malinowski.

How far can you categorise the extracts according to *purpose*?

Try to establish a purpose for each: what are people using the language *for*, in the various situations?

When you have finished, think about your own experiences of spoken language over the last 24 hours – the different *speech events* you have been involved in.

Make a list of some of the ways you have used spoken language during this time: what have you used speech for, and to whom? It will help you to tabulate some of your points. The details for one speech event has been filled in, to start you off:

Speech Events	*Purpose*	*Participants*
phone call	apology	myself and friend
(made by me)	(for not being able to meet up as planned)	

♦ ♦ ♦

FURTHER ACTIVITY II

Look in more detail at your notes on the *purposes* of the 20 extracts of spoken data. Were some much easier to categorise than others? If so, why?

Also analyse some of the different *speech events* you have been engaged in during the last two days.

Were there some types of interaction that cropped up more frequently than others?

What were the most and least common types of speech events to occur?

Why were some speech events more common than others, in your opinion?

♦ ♦ ♦

FURTHER ACTIVITY III

What follows are some examples of different spoken genres, or speech events. Read through each one, and consider the questions attached. Make some notes either in preparation for feedback to the whole group, or for your own file.

1. Here are two speeches delivered by Margaret Thatcher. The first is an extract from a speech about plans for education reform; the second is a whole speech delivered during the Falklands War.

How does the speaker use language to persuade the audience?

How do the speeches differ from spontaneous talk?

CONSERVATIVE PARTY CONFERENCE 1988

For our purpose as Conservatives/is to extend opportunity/and choice/to those who have so far been denied them/and Mr President/the task of this parliament/is to raise the quality of education/having heard what Mr Kenneth Baker/had to say about it/in that most interesting/stimulating debate/we had the other day/it's in the national interest/and it's in the individual interest/of every parent/and above all/in the interest of every child/we want education/to be part of the answer/to Britain's problems/not part of the cause/to compete successfully in tomorrow's world/against Japan/ Germany/and the United States/we need well educated/well travelled/creative young people/because if education/is backward today/national performance/will be backward tomorrow/but it's the plight/of individual boys and girls/that worries me most/too often our children/don't get the education they need/the education they deserve/and in the inner cities/where youngsters must have a decent education/if they are to have a better future/that opportunity/is too often snatched from them/by hard-left education authorities/and extremist teachers/and children who should be learning/to count and multiply/are learning anti-racist mathematics/whatever that may be/children who need to be able/to express themselves in English/are being taught political slogans/children who need to be taught/to respect traditional moral values/are being taught/that it is their inalienable right/to be gay

LORD MAYOR'S BANQUET GUILDHALL 1982

My Lord Mayor/one year ago/indeed/one momentous year ago/I talked to you about the need/for all of us to work/for one free world/the common threads that bind us/in one strong/united/West/transcend all national interests/for if political freedom/ economic efficiency/and individual vitality/were lost/then humanity/would enter its darkest age/there would be no escape/to some remaining oasis of freedom/I am sometimes asked/what does the future hold/I cannot tell you for sure/this year/any more than last/but of this I am sure/if we are strong in defence/if we are sound in finance/if we stand by/our friends and allies/if we uphold liberty/ under the law/if we encourage/the habit of enterprise/if we cultivate/a sense of personal responsibility/if we have faith in ourselves/then we can be confident/that we shall surmount/whatever problems lie ahead/confident/that we shall have/in Emerson's words/strength/still equal to the time/still swift to execute the policy/which the mind and heart of mankind/require/at the present hour/the architects of the alliance/were men of true vision/they had a dream/that the civilisation we enjoy/with its accent/on those human rights/which neither state nor man/should be able to set aside/should one day extend/to all peoples/and be handed on/to all generations/they knew/that to accomplish these great things/we must make our own defences sure/and we must proclaim/the virtues and values of liberty/the world over/let us resolve today/to do both

2. Here is an extract from an English lesson involving a group of Year 7 pupils reading and discussing a poem about fog with their teacher.

What aspects of spoken language suggest that the dialogue is from the teaching situation in general, and from English in particular?

Explore particularly the teacher's use of questioning: why do his questions not elicit any lengthy responses from the pupils?

T = teacher;   P1 = Joanne;   P2 = James;   P3 = Frances

T: Frances/stand up/read out loud/(pupil reads poem) good/right/sit down/(teacher repeats the reading of the poem) right/Joanne/why does the fog move slowly/why slowly/go on
P1: um
T: well what does slowly mean
P1: um
T: why does the fog move slowly
P2: because
T: go on/James
P2: um

T: why slowly/why not quickly
P2: because fog moves slow
T: because fog moves slowly/right/tell me/what does fog do/Frances/what does fog do to things
P3: makes things/like almost invisible
T: makes things invisible/good/then why do we say/hunch shouldered/what does that mean/if you see something/hunch shouldered/what does that mean/OK/what does that mean/Frances
P3: hugged up/snugged up/ready to strike
T: ready to strike/that's good/why is it
P3: well/cats always do/like hunch up/when they're going to pounce
T: good/good/a man called Eliot/wrote a poem/about fog/and he described it/as a cat being hunch shouldered/good/why then hunched/what does it mean/what does hunch shouldered/what kind of vision does it make/what kind of picture does it make/in your mind

3. The following is a telephone conversation between an insurance agent and a caller phoning to arrange car insurance for himself, to cover the car he is going to buy.

Why are there misunderstandings during the conversation? Try to pinpoint particular stages in the dialogue where confusions arise.

Could you apply Grice's *Maxims of Conversation* (pp.56–57) to this dialogue, to identify what the speakers are doing wrong?

A = agent;   B = caller

A: right/who introduced you to us/sir
B: sorry/I beg your pardon
A: oh/you're going to have to speak up/I'm afraid/it's very noisy
B: Mrs Sheila Leone
A: oh/it's a name you're giving me
B: yes/that's the name/you asked who introduced me/to your your company
A: does she have a policy with us
B: yes/same car/but er/I'm buying the car from her
A: right/just find the source code then/sir
B: 45/Whitefield Gardens/Whiteacre Gardens
A: I/it's OK sir/I'm just/right/so it's for Mr
B: no/it's not for/that's the woman/Mrs er whatsername/Leone/that's the person
A: so it's for Mrs L/and her surname/sir
B: mine
A: no/the/who I
B: Le Leone
A: oh/that's her surname
B: that's/that's her surname/Sheila Leone
A: oh/I'm with you now/I'm sorry/sir
B: OK
A: S/Leone
B: Sheila Leone
A: L/e/o could you tell me/how to spell it/please
B: (talking to someone in the background) how do you spell/that Sheila Leone bit/L/e/o/n/e

A: n/e/thank you/right/and her address/please
B: address is 45
A: 45
B: Whiteacre Gardens
A: Whiteacre
B: yes
A: could/w/h/i/t/e
B: w/h/i/t/e
A: a/c/r/e
B: that's right a/c/r/e
A: Garden
B: Gardens
A: Gardens
B: South Norwood
A: South Norwood/is that Croydon/Surrey
B: yes/probably/I mean/I'm from Kent/so I wouldn't really know
A: South Norwood
B: yes/I think/just put it down/as South Nor Norwood/London/when when I address letters/South East 25
A: ah/so it's South Norwood/South Norwood/London
B: I think it's 25 South/but I'm not sure
A: London
B: South West/South East 25
B: South East 25/do you have a postcode
B: do I have a postcode
A: does she have a postcode
B: I don't know/love/I don't know
A: you don't know your postcode
B: no/it's not my postcode/it's her postcode
A: oh/um
B: these are the particulars/of the Sheila Leone
A: I see/yes/it's just that I need a postcode/you see/I have to/can I look it up/and ring you back
(B talks to someone in the background)
B: 8/R/U
A: oh/sorry/8
B: yep
A: 8
B: R
A: R/for Robert
B: yes
A: U
B: yes
A: yes
B: that's right
A: is that it
B: that's it/yes
A: OK/do you have a phone numb/a phone number for her
B: do I have a phone number for her
A: does she have a phone number
B: 892
A: so it's 081/is it
B: double 2
A: 081

B: start again/I mean/you're fro/you're in London/aren't you
A: no/I'm not in London/sir
B: where you're phoning from now
A: no/I'm not in London
B: where are you phon/where am I phoning to now
A: Camberley
B: Cam where
A: Camberley
B: oh/so it'd be 081
A: is it a London
B: would it be/would it be 081/from you to London
A: yes
B: OK/put that/081/892
A: yes
B: double 2
A: yes
B: 04
A: 04/thank you very much sir/right/and her present insurance/do you know when it expires
B: well/I don't know that either/I don't know that
A: oh
B: I'm not interested/I'm not interested in her insurance/I'm interested in getting a quote/for myself
A: for yourself

4. The following are three openings from oral anecdotes related by speakers who were asked to tell a story.

How are these beginnings typical of the way we start stories in speech?

a) A while ago some friends of mine were sort of messing about with a ouija board . . .
b) When I was working at Norwood colliery there was er four men who were working along with me . . .
c) Last week Jeremy told me this story that his aunty er was coming home from the supermarket . . .

5. The following texts are all attempts by writers to represent spoken language. Now that you have studied many different aspects of real speech, you will be better able to see the strategies employed by the various writers below.

Read the texts and consider the strategies that the various writers have used to represent speech.

How do the various representations differ from real spoken language?

Why have the writers chosen to represent speech as they have?

a) In this extract from *Wuthering Heights* by Emily Brontë, Joseph, the Yorkshire manservant, has prepared some food for the young child, Linton. Linton has refused to eat it.

'Cannot ate it?' repeated Joseph, peering in Linton's face, and subduing his voice to a whisper, for fear of being overheard. 'But Maister Hareton nivir ate naught else, when he wer a little un; and what were gooid eneugh for him's gooid eneugh for ye. Aw's rayther think!'

'I *shan't* eat it!' answered Linton snappishly. 'Take it away'.

Joseph snatched up the food indignantly, and brought it to us.

'Is there aught ails th' victuals?' he asked, thrusting the tray under Heathcliffe's nose.

'What should ail them?' he said.

'Wah!' answered Joseph, 'yon dainty chap says he cannut ate 'em. But Aw guess it's raight! His mother wer just soa – we wer a'most too mucky to sow t'corn for makking her breead'.

b) In this extract from *Tess of the D'Urbervilles* by Thomas Hardy, which is set in the West Country, Tess's mother has had a letter from their rich, distant relatives, the D'Urbervilles, offering Tess a job.

When she entered the house she perceived in a moment from her mother's triumphant manner that something had occurred in the interim.

'Oh yes; I know all about it! I told 'ee it would be all right, and now 'tis proved!'

'Since I've been away? What has?' said Tess rather wearily.

Her mother surveyed the girl up and down with arch approval, and went on banteringly: 'So you've brought 'em round!'

'How do you know, mother?'

'I've had a letter.'

Tess then remembered that there would have been time for this.

'They say – Mrs. D'Urberville says – that she wants you to look after a little fowl-farm which is her hobby. But this is only her artful way of getting 'ee there without raising your hopes. She's going to own 'ee as kin – that's the meaning o't.'

'But I didn't see her.'

'You zid somebody, I suppose?'

'I saw her son.'

'And did he own 'ee?'

'Well – he called me Coz.'

'An I knew it! Jacky – he called her Coz!' cried Joan to her husband. 'Well, he spoke to his mother, of course, and she do want 'ee there.'

'But I don't know that I am apt at tending fowls,' said the dubious Tess.

'Then I don't know who is apt. You've be'n born in the business, and brought up in it. They that be born in a business always know more about it than any 'prentice. Besides, that's only just a show of something for you to do, that you midn't feel beholden.'

c) An extract from 'Coronation Street'

(Cut to Snug: Kevin and Sally. He has a lager, she has a shandy.)

SALLY: 'Ey, do you know a girl called Susan Clayton, she says she knows you.

KEVIN: (Thinks) Susan . . . you don't mean little Sue Clayton, by any chance, do yer?

SALLY: Works in a bakery down Everton Street.

KEVIN: (Grins) Aye, that'll be 'er. She allus was a little pest with big ideas. Used to live up the road. 'Er skin an' blister 'ad a thing with Terry. Well, more'n a thing, it were a 'ole big drama. (Then) Why, anyroad?

SALLY: I went for an interview there. Got chattin' while I was waitin'. She says it's not bad but she can't see 'erself makin' Eccles cakes for't rest of 'er life.

KEVIN: (Teasing) 'Ey, be brill, that. I like Eccles cakes!

SALLY: (Sarcastically) Oh, well, in that case I'll definitely take the job, if they offer it me.

KEVIN: (Serious now) Wouldn't you anyway?

SALLY: (Sighs, she's really down) I s'pose so. Be summat to do. Honest sometimes I get that cheesed off. I wake up in't mornin' an' think 'Why bother gerrin' up? What's to gerrup *for*?'

KEVIN: (Light, trying to cheer her up) Me?

SALLY: I'm serious, Kev. It's different for you. You've go'rra job you *like*. I've nor'even go'rra *job*.

◆ ◆ ◆

4. Asking Questions

Language is something we all know about and use; but it should be clear to you by now that, within language, there is a very wide range of different areas to study. You will also have realised that even within one area – such as spoken language – there are many specific and different aspects that can be looked at. In order to ask a question about language, you have to focus on a particular area to ask that question about.

This unit aims to do two things; first, to help you see a variety of ways in which language can be divided up, so that it is easier to ask questions that you will be able to answer; second, to help you think about the different sorts of questions that you can ask.

On p.70 is a table which shows a possible way to divide up language study into different *language levels* and *language areas*.

LANGUAGE LEVELS are the different ingredients of language that you explored in the decoding sections of this book. They are as follows:

Phonology: the sound system of language

Graphology: the system of written symbols in language

Semantics: the system of meaning created by words and phrases used

Grammar: the system of language structures

Discourse: the way whole language interactions or texts work. This level is the larger one which may include some or all of the other levels of language.

LANGUAGE AREAS are very broad subjects or topics which often form the basis of whole courses. They are as follows:

Language Acquisition: This covers the way in which we learn language, regardless of whether we are learning our first language or second, and regardless of what age we are. If we are learning the system of any language as part of the natural process of interacting with others in society, then we are acquiring it, or 'picking it up'; sometimes, the terms 'language learning' or 'language development' are used to refer to the more self-conscious process where language is not simply 'picked up', but consciously learned. Either way, we all acquire or learn something of the range of language levels outlined above.

	Language Acquisition (Picking up Language)	Language Change (Changes in Time)	Language Varieties (Differences)	Language and Society (Attitudes)
Phonological level	Acquisition of sounds	Changes in the sound system	Differences between sound systems	Attitudes to acquisition of, changes in, and differences between, sound systems and their uses
Graphological level	Acquisition of written symbols and other graphological conventions	Changes in graphological conventions	Differences between graphological conventions	Attitudes to acquisition of, changes in, and differences between, graphological conventions and their uses
Semantic level	Acquisition of vocabulary and meanings	Changes in word meanings; invention and loss of terms	Differences between vocabulary used by or about individuals or groups	Attitudes to acquisition of, changes in, and differences between, vocabulary systems and their uses
Grammatical level	Acquisition of grammatical structures	Changes in grammatical structures	Differences between grammatical structures	Attitudes to acquisition of, changes in, and differences between, grammatical systems and their uses
Discourse level	Acquisition of a range of language functions (e.g. to entertain; to persuade) and spoken/written genres (e.g. oral narrative; written letter)	Changes in whole spoken/written genres	Differences between whole spoken/written genres; variations within a genre	Attitudes to acquisition of, changes in, and differences between, spoken/written genres and their uses

Language Change: This covers the way in which language changes over the course of time: all aspects of language are subject to change, but the most noticeable aspect is change in word usage, with words dying out or changing their meanings, and new words being invented to describe new ideas and objects.

Language Varieties: This covers the ways in which language varies; according to such large-scale factors as region, age, gender, social class, and occupation, influencing the language use of whole groups of people for long periods of time; and also according to smaller-scale factors, such as the relative status of speakers or writers, their setting, the purpose and topic of the conversation or text, and whether speech or writing is being used. These factors influence the way individuals vary their language over relatively short periods of time.

Language and Society: This covers our attitudes to language, including such aspects as the status we give to particular groups and types of language; the way we stereotype others by their language use; and our various language 'taboos' which reflect the areas of experience we feel uncomfortable about.

INITIAL ACTIVITY

Look at the data below.

What area on the table is each piece of language an example of?

Try to match each example with at least one of the boxes.

(You may decide that some of the examples could cover more than one box.)

1.
> little bonkey
> little bonkey on
> the busty road
> got to keep
> Plobbind ohwarb on
> with your Presioys
> loaves

2. ba ba bæk tip
   (Baa baa black sheep)

3.

4.

Simon's progress this year has been rather poor.

5. ʃjuʈ (suit)   ɔf (off)

6.

If anything can keep him off the golf course
long enough to help dry up, it's a gay Old Bleach
pure linen cloth.   Equip yourself with the new
heavier weight kitchen cloths as well as the original
rainbow-striped glass cloths.   Both *ready for use*
— soft and absorbent without previous washing.

OLD BLEACH *ready to dry*
kitchen and glass cloths
OLD BLEACH LINEN CO LTD RANDALSTOWN N . IRELAND

7. We was going down the road, like.

8.  Ruth, aged 4, describing pins and needles in her legs: 'I've got fizzy legs.'

9. bæθ (bath)   kʊp (cup)

10.

Reprimand for Aids language

By James Lewis

A BBC Wales radio producer has been reprimanded and is now on leave because a programme on Aids included what the corporation said were 'earthy and coarse' descriptions of homosexual acts.

The Welsh language programme, called Manylu, included an interview with a homosexual who, according to a BBC spokesman, used 'extremely coarse language to describe acts which might cause one to contract Aids'. Although there were no complaints from listeners, the controller of BBC Wales, Mr Gareth Price, decided to broadcast an apology for the use of 'totally unacceptable' words.

The producer, Delyth Ennaf Davies, is understood to have been reprimanded because she refused to remove the offending words from a repeat broadcast and because she had failed to refer upwards the content of a sensitive programme before it was broadcast.

First published in *The Guardian* (James Lewis)

11.

Between you and I, Jane was invited as well as myself. I expect you was invited too!

Shamed By Your Mistakes In English?

Many people use such expressions as "Jane was invited as well as myself", and "was you going tonight?"

Still others say "between you and I" instead of "between you and me". It is astonishing how often "who" is used for "whom" and how frequently we hear such glaring mispronunciations as "tomorrER" and "reservOY". Few know whether to spell certain words with one or two "r's" or "m's" or with "ei" or "ie".

Indeed thousands of talented, intelligent people are held back at work and socially because their command of English does not equal their other abilities.

For example, most people do not realise how much they could influence others simply by speaking and writing with greater power, authority and precision. Whether you are presenting a report, training a child, fighting for a cause, making a sale, writing an essay, or asking for a rise . . . your success depends upon the words you use.

And now the right words are yours to command! A free book. "Good English — the Language of Success", tells you all about a remarkable, new home-study course which can give you a swift mastery of good English in just 20 minutes a day.

Never again need you fear those embarrassing mistakes. You can quickly and easily be shown how to ensure that everything you say and write is crisp, clear, *correct.*

This amazing self-training method will show you how to double your powers of self-expression, giving you added poise, self-confidence and greater personal effectiveness. You will discover how you can dominate each situation whether at home, at work, or even in casual conversation with new acquaintances. You will learn how to increase your vocabulary, speed up your reading, enhance your powers of conversation, and tremendously improve your grammar, writing and speaking — all in your spare time at home.

What's more, you will command the respect of people who matter, because you'll learn how to use English accurately, impressively, incisively — to cut through many barriers to social, academic or business success.

For your free copy of "Good English — the Language of Success", and proof that this unique home-study method really works, simply post the coupon on Page — NOW. You have nothing to lose, not even a postage stamp, and you may gain a great deal by sending for this free book. For your own sake post the coupon TODAY. Or write to Practical English Programme, (Dept. IDE31, TMD FREEPOST, London WC2E 9BR.

12.

I WONDER how many others become as incensed as I do when listening to the radio or watching television (newsreaders in particular) with regard to the correct vowel sound "oo" (as in the words do, rude, or mood).

How do these people obtain their particular job? Surely they should know what shape the lips should be to emit this particular vowel. It is so irritating to hear something like "de-u" for "do" etc. It is not their accent which is wrong (it is usually good old BBC accent) but why cannot announcers in such privileged positions learn to pronounce this vowel correctly?

I usually find that Southerners are the worst offenders. Although having perfect delivery, enunciation, pronunciation (in other respects), this one irritating fault (and fault it is) still persists. If anyone genuinely is interested in overcoming this fault (which perhaps they are) I would be only too pleased to help them.
Qualified helper, Stockport.

First published in the *Manchester Evening News*

Check your findings against the answers on p.75.

If you have been working in pairs, share your results with others in the whole group – how far do you agree on the areas covered by the language data?

✦✦✦

FURTHER ACTIVITY I

Look back at the table again on p.70.

A table like this can be useful in helping you to see how the different *language levels* could be the focus for a piece of research within the broad *language areas*.

Read through the list of Topic Outlines on p.76.

These outlines have been taken from 'A' Level Language research projects written by students during the last few years.

For each outline, decide which boxes on the table you would fit the outline into – what do you think the *main focus* was for each project? One project may well cover a number of different language levels, so don't feel you have to fit each outline into one box only.

In particular, you may find that you want to mark the discourse level as well as the smaller levels that go to make it up.

Answers (Initial Activity p.71)

1. Language Acquisition – Graphology

2. Language Acquisition – Phonology

3. Language Change – Grammar (Everyone . . . their)

4. Language Varieties – Graphology/Semantics/Grammar/Discourse (Occupational Language)

5. Language Change – Phonology (Changes in the RP accent)

6. Language Change – Semantics ('gay Old Bleach')

7. Language Varieties and Society (Dialect vocabulary and grammar and attitudes to this)

8. Language Acquisition – Semantics

9. Language Varieties – Phonology (Northern pronunciations)

10. Language and Society – Semantics (Attitudes to taboo vocabulary)

11. Language and Society – Phonology/Semantics/Grammar (Attitudes to regional language and 'correctness')

12. Language and Society – Phonology (Attitudes to change in RP pronunciation)

TOPIC OUTLINES

1. A study of the pronunciation of an eight year-old boy who has been referred to the speech therapist.

2. A comparison between the accent spoken in North Lincolnshire, and Received Pronunciation.

3. An examination of the use of swear words by groups of students of different genders. I intend to explore the differences in usage, and to try to find reasons for the existence of any differences I discover.

4. An exploration of how language is used between counter staff and customers in food outlets.

5. A comparison of newspaper stories from *The Times* in the years 1920 and 1988.

6. A study of grafitti in different city centre venues.

7. An exploration of the spoken language of the Courts.

8. A study of the conversational rules in family interactions during meal-times.

9. A study of the language use of Afro-Caribbean speakers.

10. An examination of the development of children's narrative skills in writing; a comparison of stories written by seven year olds and eleven year olds.

11. A comparison between spoken and written instructions.

12. An analysis of a number of descriptions of sexual encounters in different literary texts.

13. A study of the techniques used in a range of contemporary magazine adverts for cars.

14. An analysis of the use and importance of personal names.

15. An examination of the way in which people stereotype others by their accents. I intend to record a number of differently-accented speakers, and ask informants to respond to the different accents.

16. An analysis of a number of TV adult game shows, to establish whether there is a formula being followed.

17. A comparison between 'Watch with Mother' (a children's TV programme from the 1950s) and a modern children's programme.

18. Songs of Protest: an analysis of song lyrics by different artists aiming to register political protest.

19. A study of the language of gravestones, with particular reference to euphemisms about death.

20. An analysis of the language of crossword clues.

21. A comparison of problem pages from magazines written in 1930 and 1988.

22. An analysis of a range of political speeches given at Party Conferences.

(Answers are given on p.78.)

If you have been working in groups, feed back your results to the group as a whole, while checking your answers.

How far are you in agreement about the areas and levels that would have been covered by the projects?

◆ ◆ ◆

FURTHER ACTIVITY II

Now look again at the three Topic Outlines below.

If the outlines had been the versions in italics, what different levels or areas would the researchers have had to explore?

2. A comparison between the accent spoken in North Lincolnshire, and Received Pronunciation.
   A comparison between the dialect of North Lincolnshire, and Standard English.

13. A study of the techniques used in a range of contemporary magazine adverts for cars.
    A comparison of a number of car adverts – two from 1952 and two from 1990.

16. An analysis of a number of TV adult game shows, to establish whether there is a formula being followed.
    A comparison of two news programmes, one aimed at adults, and the other at children.

(Answers are given on p.79.)

◆ ◆ ◆

FURTHER ACTIVITY III

Each group or individual should take one of the language areas you have been studying (repeated on p.79).

Draw a tree diagram which outlines some of the options possible in that area. For each area, a number of options have been given to help you; add any further options which come to you during the course of your work.

Try to give your tree diagram as many branches as you can, to cover all the options you can think of. If you decide you have exhausted your diagram, but can still think of more possibilities, draw some more diagrams. This activity is intended to be a brainstorm to give you ideas, rather than a neat and tidy exercise which will give you all the answers – so don't worry if your work ends up looking messy.

ANSWERS (FURTHER ACTIVITY I p.75)

(N.B. Your decisions on levels may vary – in practice, this would depend on the precise nature of the data that had been collected)

Areas	*Possible Levels*
1. Language Acquisition	Phonology
2. Language Varieties	Phonology
3. Language Varieties and Society	Semantics
4. Language Varieties	Phonology, Semantics, Grammar, Discourse
5. Language Change	Graphology, Semantics, Grammar, Discourse
6. Language Varieties	Graphology, Semantics, Grammar, Discourse
7. Language Varieties	Phonology, Semantics, Grammar, Discourse
8. Language Varieties	Phonology, Semantics, Grammar, Discourse
9. Language Varieties	Phonology, Semantics, Grammar
10. Language Acquisition	Discourse (+ possibly Graphology, Semantics and Grammar)
11. Language Varieties	All levels
12. Language Varieties	Semantics, Grammar, Discourse
13. Language Varieties	Graphology, Semantics, Grammar, Discourse
14. Language Varieties and Society	Semantics
15. Language and Society	Phonology
16. Language Varieties	Discourse
17. Language Change	Phonology, Semantics, Grammar, Discourse
18. Language Varieties	Phonology, Semantics, Grammar, Discourse
19. Language Varieties	Semantics as main focus
20. Language Varieties	Graphology, Semantics, Grammar, Discourse
21. Language Change	Graphology, Semantics, Grammar, Discourse
22. Language Varieties	Discourse (+ Phonology, Semantics, Grammar)

Language Area	*Options*
Language Acquisition	Adults or children? One individual or many? Typical development or not? Language features or functions? Speech or writing?
Language Change	Speech or writing? One language level or more? Literary material or not?
Language Varieties	One individual or many? One social factor or more (age, gender, occupation, region, class, etc.)? Speech or writing? Literary material or not? One genre or a comparison?
Language and Society	Attitudes to which other language area (acquisition, change, varieties)? One level or more?

If you have been working in groups, each group in turn should pin up their tree diagram(s) and explain to the other groups the various options they discussed and drew for their language area.

When you have finished, consider the following questions:

● Have the activities you have completed so far helped you to understand more about the language areas and levels you could research?

● Have there been any aspects of the work you have done in this unit that have confused you?

Discuss these as a whole group if you are in a group situation; if you are working alone, make some notes on issues you would like to clarify, and discuss these at the next meeting with your supervisor.

ANSWERS (FURTHER ACTIVITY II p.77)

2. Language Varieties – vocabulary and grammar, rather than phonology

13. Language Change – same levels as before

16. Language Varieties – the focus would be less on the 'rules' of the genre (discourse) and more on variations in vocabulary and grammar to accommodate the different audiences

Different Types of Question

The ordinary questions that you use in everyday conversation are also the questions that are relevant for research purposes.

Ordinary question words are: what; how; why; when; where; and who.

Whatever area or level of language you decide to research, the following are going to be relevant questions to ask:

WHAT? Researchers will always want to know 'What happens?' After getting a focus on an area to explore, a researcher will need to find some data, or raw material, to give him or her some evidence of what happens in that area.

HOW? A part of every investigation will be 'How does it work?' Whatever the research question, and whatever the data that has been collected, the researcher will want to know how the data 'works' – how it hangs together, whether there are patterns to be observed, what the 'rules' are.

WHY? The two questions above lead naturally to a third question – 'Why does it happen like this?' The researcher will always want to ask what the language tells us about the human beings behind it: what are they trying to do; what are their motives and concerns; what factors are working on them, to make them behave in this way?

Aside from the question above, you may also want to ask other questions, depending on the area of language being researched:

WHEN? When does/did this language use occur?

WHERE? Is this language use particular to a certain geographical or social area?

WHO? Are there certain individuals or groups who use this type of language?

FURTHER ACTIVITY IV

In order to test out the usefulness of the questions you have just been reading about, read through the data on pp.81–82.

The data was collected as follows: *Menu A* is from a transport cafe on the outskirts of Manchester; *Menu B* is from a large chain hotel in Newcastle upon Tyne.

First, decide what your research question will be. Look back at the table of language areas and levels (p.70) to help you to decide the main area and levels you will be covering.

Apply each of the questions: what? how? and why? in turn to the data, and write down some brief notes, either for your own file or for feedback to the whole group.

Then decide whether any of the questions: when? where? and who? are relevant to your study.

When you have finished, consider the following further questions:

● How useful were the questions: what? how? and why? Do you think these questions are always going to be relevant to language research?

● Which of the questions: when? where? and who? were relevant to what you were doing? Can you think of areas of language which would involve the questions that you didn't use?

MENU A

WAYFARER CAFE

ALL DAY FULL B/FAST WITH B/B
OR TOAST, INC POT TEA
HOMEMADE + 2 VEG, POTS
STEAK + KIDNEY, ALL IN
HOT-POT
HAM SHANK, CHIPS OR JACKET
LIVER + ONIONS
YORKSHIRES/MUSHY PEAS/BLACK PUD EXTRA

APPLE PIE + CUSTARD
BAKEWELL TART
PARKIN

VARIOUS SNACKS
SAUSAGE MUFFIN
BACON BARM
SCOLLOPS + GRAVY
CHIPS + GRAVY/CURRY SAUCE
OR TO ORDER

MENU B

THE RAVENSCROFT SUITE:
GOURMET DINNER DANCE

An interesting warm salad of smoked bacon, wild mushrooms and duck, quickly cooked and abound with a melange of winter leaves sprinkled in a walnut dressing

★

Peeled prawns bound in a tomato enhanced mayonnaise with diced pineapple and walnuts, nestled on a meli-melo of lettuce served in a glass

★

A collection of cured meats and poultry, nestled on a rustic salad and doused in a warm raspberry dressing

★

A terrine of fresh vegetables, sliced onto a coulis of tomato and fresh herbs

★ ★ ★

Supreme of fresh salmon attentively grilled, presented on a cushion of homemade noodles with a champagne sauce

★ ★ ★

Fillets of fresh monkfish spread with a mousse of scampi caressed in cabbage and poached, sliced onto a dry vermouth and avocado sauce

★ ★ ★

Medallions of pork pan-fried and masked in a pink peppercorn sauce accompanied by caramelized kumquats

★ ★ ★

Escalope of turkey folded with cranberry sauce, dusted in breadcrumbs and baked, escorted by a rich Madeira sauce

★ ★ ★

Rounds of venison quickly pan-fried and masked with a sharp blackcurrant sauce with just a suspicion of Juniper berry

★ ★ ★

A tournedos of beef topped with a liver parfait, enrobed in crepinette and oven-baked, served with a Madeira and truffle fondue

◆ ◆ ◆

5. Methods Of Data Collection, Organisation and Transcription

This unit aims to get you thinking about the different ways you can collect language data, and the best ways to present your data so that your reader is clear about what you were trying to do and what you have found.

Methods of Data Collection

A. WHAT IS DATA?

Data is the raw material of a language research project. It is the material you collect in your attempt to answer the question you have posed yourself in the original aim of your project.

Where you look for your data will be determined by your aim, but there are a variety of ways to collect data, and methods of data collection need careful consideration before you start. People whom you use as part of your research project are called *informants*.

B. COLLECTING SPOKEN DATA

Here are some different ways to collect spoken language:

Note-making: This is where you write notes on what is being said.

Questionnaires on self-reported usage: This is where you ask individuals to tell you about the language that they use. You may ask informants verbally about their language, and write their responses down yourself, or you may simply give them a form to fill in on their own.

Tape-recordings with the participants' knowledge: Informants know that you are recording them, but you may tell them that you are looking for something other than your real aim. You may be recording a variety of different types of events – informants reading from word lists or set passages; informants producing monologues about particular subjects; interviews; a number of informants involved in a dialogue.

Tape-recordings without the participants' knowledge: Informants are not aware of being recorded; after you have obtained your recording you are legally obliged to ask their permission to use the data. As above, you may be recording any one of many different situations.

Regardless of whether informants know they are being recorded or not, you, as speaker and researcher, have to make a decision about how far to be involved in any interaction.

Recordings taken from media sources – for example, radio and TV programmes – also do not involve participant awareness of your particular recording, although obviously speakers were aware of the situation of the original recording or transmission. You, as a researcher, are not involved in any way in the interaction.

INITIAL ACTIVITY

Consider the different methods described above, and, for each, write some notes on what you see as its strengths and weaknesses. Think about the practical aspects of collecting speech, as well as the possible warping factors involved in each method. Tabulate your ideas, using three columns:

Research Method   *Strengths*   *Weaknesses*

When you have finished, assess your ideas on the different methods described:

● Have you found clear patterns of strengths and weaknesses?

● Are there any further methods that have not been mentioned?

◆ ◆ ◆

FURTHER ACTIVITY

Go back to the list of Topic Outlines you considered in *Unit 4* (p.76).

Concentrate only on the projects that involve the analysis of *speech*. For each of these projects, say which method of data collection would be best.

Write some detailed notes on your choice of method, and any particular problems that you think could arise. Where projects involve media texts, discuss how you would decide which programmes to record.

When you have finished, compare your results with those of the other groups, if you have been working in a group situation.

How far do you agree on the methods for each of the projects on spoken language? Where you disagree, try to establish the issues involved which triggered your different choices. It may well be that different methods would work, depending on which particular aspects of language were being explored.

If you have been working alone, compare your ideas with the actual methods used (listed on p.85). Constructively criticise the actual methods used.

◆ ◆ ◆

C. COLLECTING WRITTEN DATA

In some ways, written texts are much easier to collect than spoken ones, because of the practical problems involved in recording spoken language. But collecting written language needs careful preparation and attention too, in order to make sure that the data is suited to the question being asked, and in order to arrive at the right amount of material.

INITIAL ACTIVITY

Look at the Topic Outlines again (p.76), this time focusing on those projects that involve the analysis of *writing*, or where data could be drawn from both *speech* and *writing*.

For each project, decide what would be the important factors to consider in the collection of written material (or the spoken and written material).

For example:
— should the subject matter of the writing be kept constant for some of the projects, and, if so, why? How can this be achieved?
— when the outline mentions a 'range', 'group', 'number', or just uses a plural and doesn't specify a number, how large a range should that be?
— should the items or people in the range or group differ from each other in some way?

When you have finished, pool your ideas on the important factors to consider when collecting written language, if you have been working in a group situation. If you have been working alone, compare your ideas with the factors outlined on p.86.

♦ ♦ ♦

Notes (Further Activity p.84)

Collecting Spoken Data

Topic Outline (p.76)	Methods of Data Collection Used
1	Tape recording with participant's knowledge
2	As No. 1
3	Questionnaires on self-reported usage
4	Tape recording without participants' knowledge
7	Note-making (tape recording in court is illegal)
8	As in No. 1
9	As in No. 1
15	As in No. 1, then questionnaires given to informants
16	Recording from different TV channels – three programmes
17	Recording from TV of one programme aimed at similar age group to 'Watch With Mother'
18	Three songs centring on specific issue – racism
22	Recording of two speeches – one Labour/one Conservative

Data Organisation

READABILITY

Any piece of language research is not simply an exploration for your own interest, although, obviously, that is an important element of your work. It should also, as a piece of communication in its own right, be accessible to any interested reader. For that reason, you need to give some thought to how your data should be presented and organised. This is not merely about where to place the raw data in your project; it is also about how your findings should appear. For this reason, issues about organisation should be considered at the outset and all the way through the process of research, not just at the final, 'fair copy' stage.

INITIAL ACTIVITY ▮ or ▮▮▮

Look at the pieces of dialogue on pp.87–88, from radio phone-in programmes.

Imagine that your research was to explore how address terms were used between the callers and the DJs/studio 'expert'.

You want to show your reader what terms of address were used and by whom, as part of your project on *language and gender*.

NOTES (INITIAL ACTIVITY p.85)

Collecting Written or Spoken and Written Data

Topic Outline (p.76)	Factors for Consideration
5	Content needs to be the same or similar – three small stories covered by actual project, on theme of royal occasions
6	Venues need to be clearly different in nature – three venues used by actual project
10	Stories need to be on the same or similar subject – five stories chosen from each group by actual researcher
11	Instructions need to be for the same type of activity
12	Useful if different approaches taken by the texts – three texts used in actual project
13	Useful if texts show different techniques – four texts chosen by actual project
14	Range of data needed – newspapers plus questionnaires on self-reported attitudes used by actual project
19	Selection important, if want to concentrate on semantics as main focus
20	Two different crosswords used by actual project to show variety of techniques
21	Useful if content can be similar – two problem pages chosen by actual project

Devise a *table* to show the use of address terms in this data. Your aim is to enable your reader to grasp any patterns evident in the data. The table is not intended to replace written analysis, but to support it by enabling your reader to see quickly what was going on in the dialogues.

DATA

Competition phone-in: Guess the mystery voice.

Competitor – Dave

DJ: Is Julie there?
Dave: No she's out.
DJ: Who's that?
Dave: Her brother, Dave Grimley.
DJ: Well, let's have a few hellos to your chums. The wireless is yours, sir.
(Dave says hello to some of his friends).
DJ: What do you do, then?
Dave: I'm unemployed.
DJ: What do you want?
Dave: A job.
DJ: Of *course* you want a job, my son. But what?
(Dave talks about a designing job).
DJ: Be a little more specific, Dave, baby.
(DJ plays the mystery voice).
DJ: You haven't got a clue, have you, Dave? Here's ten seconds thinking time, but I don't suppose it'll do you much good, will it?

Competitor – Iris

DJ: Is Iris there?
Iris: Hello.
DJ: Iris!
Iris: Who is it?
DJ: Young cuddly Iris! Young Iris, how are you, Iris, Iris?
(DJ explains that someone has written a letter about her).
DJ: That's a letter that's bound to get you on the wireless, chuck!
(DJ shouts to Iris's daughter: How are you kid?)
(DJ tells Iris that £7 is on offer).
DJ: £7 is better than a kick in the gob, isn't it, dear?
(DJ plays voice).
DJ: Did you get that all right, dear? Come on, kid.
Iris: I haven't a clue.
DJ: Oh, Iris, Iris, have you no idea at all, chuck?
(Iris says she doesn't know).
(Losers get the consolation prize of a tee-shirt).
DJ: What size tee-shirt would you like, darling?
(Talk about Iris's family. She has a lot of children. She mentions TV)
DJ: Have you got a telly, dear?
(DJ makes some cheeky comments about how Iris gets the time to watch TV).
DJ: See you, chuck, bye-bye, love.

Phone-in programme on car problems. Greetings and farewells between callers, a DJ and a studio 'expert'.

Caller – Patricia

DJ: Good morning, sweetheart.
Expert: Good morning, Pat.
Pat: Hello . . .
DJ: Thanks for your call. Goodbye, sweetheart.

Caller – William

DJ: Hello William. Good morning, sir.
William: Good morning.
Expert: Good morning, William.
William: Good morning, Keith . . . (expert)
DJ: Bye now.

Caller – Ann

DJ: Good morning.
Ann: Good morning.
DJ: Hello, sweetheart. What's your problem?
DJ: Thanks for the call, my love (To listeners: 'She's a nice girl').

Caller – Thomas

DJ: Hellow Thomas, sir.
Expert: Hello Thomas.
Thomas: How do . . .
DJ: Thanks for your call. Bye.

If you were working in groups, share your tables with the other groups when you have finished. It is not important how neat and tidy your tables are: the crucial aspect of this activity is thinking through how to be economical and clear in your data organisation. If you were working alone, show the data and your table to a reader, and ask them to respond to the following questions:

● Is it clear what main points you were trying to make in your tables?

● Which aspects of your tables did your reader(s) find helpful/unclear?

Then consider, for your own benefit:

— what the difference is between the information you have in your tables, and the sort of points you would make in your written analysis;
— where you would put the spoken dialogues (i.e. your raw data) if this were really your project.

✦ ✦ ✦

Data Transcription

If you are attempting a project on spoken language, it is unlikely that you will want to transcribe all the material you record; your first task, then, is to *select* the parts that are most relevant to the question you are exploring. Your next decision is *how much detail to transcribe* in the data you have selected.

The purpose of transcription markings is to help the reader to recreate the spoken language in his/her own mind. A transcript should be free-standing and independent: in other words, a reader should not need to listen to the tape in order to know what is being referred to in the analysis. It is therefore important to mark those aspects of speech that are not obvious on the page. But what you decide to mark will depend on what aspect of speech your project is concerned with. For example, the transcript below (which appeared in *Unit 3*) is from a project which explored how people manage topic changes in conversations. For this reason, the researcher felt it was important to mark intonation, overlapping speech, and non-verbal behaviour, particularly eye contact.

INITIAL ACTIVITY  **or**

Read the transcript aloud and act it out physically, attempting to recreate the speech situation by using the appropriate intonation and non-verbal behaviour. If you are working alone, ask some other readers to help you to realise the dialogue.

Can you get a sense of what the conversation was like?

The dialogue took place in a queue in a sandwich shop near to a sixth form college in Manchester. The speakers are all students who know each other very well.

E = Emma, K = Kate, P = Philip, N = Nicola,
. . . = overlapping speech

E: (accelerando) `listen/ ,right/I'went to the `toilet/and we'went near this`sand pit/ ,right/and I'got úp the next`morning/and'all my`shoes/were'caked in`white stuff/ce`ment/or ,summat/(rallentando, imitating tiredness) oh`god/'what's it been like at`college then/ ,alright/I'm `knackered/ ,me/I'm'dead`tired/I can't`stand this weather/it's too `warm/*I*

K: (looking directly at Emma) *'where's* `Stephanie today

E: (returning eye contact) she'll be`here/in a ,bit/we've'got a`lesson/I ,think/ I`hope she's got a lesson/ `anyway
(Philip looks towards Emma)

P: (laughter) I'had ice-`cream/on ,there/(indicates record album he is holding) so I'licked it `off/because it was on *Ma`donna*

E: (returning eye contact) *`wooh*/`Philip

K: (looking directly at Emma) 'where did you`go/'this week`end
(Emma and Kate exchange eye contact while speaking to each other)

E: 'number`one/on'Friday`night

K: 'we went on `Saturday

E: I'didn't see anyone I`knew/on Friday ,night

K: `no/ `most of them go/on`Saturdays

E: (looking at Phil) I'went`in/and the`bouncer/was'all`over me/`wasn't he *Phil*

P: (looking at Kate) *^mmm*/ ˈthatᵛbouncer/wasˈwellˋafter *her*
E: *and* heˋwent/and he/(Emma suddenly notices Nicky standing behind them in the queue) ˋeh/weˈnearly got fuckin' chuckedˋout/of ˈthis otherˋclub/ ˌcause of ˌyou
N: (looking around her) *ˋme*
E: (looking directly at Nicola) *ˋyeah*/ˋcallin' *everyone*
P: *(laughter)*
E: (generally) ˋStephs at it/I'mˈgonnaˋkill Nicky

✦ ✦ ✦

FURTHER ACTIVITY

Look once again at the list of Topic Outlines (p.76), this time concentrating just on those that involve the analysis of spoken language.

Take each project in turn and make some notes on the particular aspects of spoken language that, in your opinion, should be marked in any data transcript.

It may be useful to refer to *Unit 3: Decoding Spoken Texts* (p.35) to help you.

Here is a list of areas that were covered in that unit:

- Intonation
- Phonemic transcription
- The speech context
- The grammar of speech
- Spoken vocabularies
- Interaction features

If you were working in a group situation, share your ideas on the types of transcription necessary for the projects on speech. Where you differ in your results, how far is this because you had differing interpretations of what the projects were trying to do?

If you were working alone, make some notes on your observations for your own use, and for discussion with your supervisor at an appropriate date.

✦ ✦ ✦

Section B

✦

BUILDING UP RESEARCH SKILLS

✦ ✦ ✦

The aim of this section is to get you familiar in more detail with some of the language areas that can be explored for research purposes. Learning how to go about research is a skill that is acquired through practice. The units in this section are designed to give you that practice, so that, after working on them, you will be much more confident about undertaking your own independent enquiries.

Each unit covers a different language area, and does the following:

- Explains briefly what the language area is concerned with
- Offers a range of language date for analysis
- Outlines different questions that could be asked about the data
- Suggests ways to start working analytically
- Gives a list of different topics that could be attempted in that area

1. Norms and Variations

As the title suggests, this area is asking about options in language use. The word 'norm' refers to what happens, as a general rule; and 'variations' refers to alternative choices that can be made.

Studies on norms and variations always look at a system of language use; a small, often closed, area where it is possible to spell out the rules and conventions.

As a researcher, your work is to find out why certain choices of language were made – what are the triggering factors? What were people trying to do with their language, when they made the choices they did?

Examples: terms of address; graffiti; the language of gravestones; names of all kinds; book titles and 'blurbs'; the language of menus; greetings cards; colour terms; connotations of particular groups of terms, e.g. 'ladies' vs. 'girls' vs. 'women'.

THE LANGUAGE OF CHOCOLATE BARS

INITIAL ACTIVITY

On p.94 is a collection of chocolate bar names. These chocolate bars were all the confectionery on display in one sweet shop in a small town on 5 September, 1992.

Consider the names given to these sweets; what do you think the manufacturers were trying to suggest, in giving their products these names? What *connotations* do they have? Are there any patterns of usage here: can you group the names into categories, where the same or a similar idea is being suggested? Here are some possible headings to work with:

shape; texture; size/quantity/value; animal names; mythical figures; planetary references; lifestyle; ingredients; stamina/success in competition; exotic locations/cultures; private pleasure

Apart from the meanings of the words, are some names similar to others *graphologically* (the way the words are spelt, the way they look), *grammatically* (the type of word chosen, e.g. noun, adjective, verb) or *phonologically* (the sounds of the words when spoken)? Create some more groupings with these different language levels in mind.

Ruffle	Double Decker
Drifter	Marathon
Wispa	Moments
Galaxy	Minstrels
Boost	Smarties
Turkish Delight	Twirl
Skittles	Bounty
Picnic	Flake
Munchies	Maltesers
Caramac	Mintolas
Aero	Lion
Milky Bar	Jamaica
Secret	Rolos
Milky Way	M&Ms
Top Ten	Ripple
Curly Wurly	Spira
Big Deal	Dime
Toffee Crisp	Crunchie
Chomp	Caramel
Walnut Whip	

When you have finished, do the same activities for the following chocolate box names

Biarritz	Milk Tray
Dairy Box	Roses
Moonlight	Black Magic
All Gold	

✦ ✦ ✦

FURTHER ACTIVITY or

Pool your categories and discuss your findings, if you were working in a group situation. Whatever your chosen method of working, consider the following:

● Were you able to find consistent patterns in the way these names work? In other words, can you see *systems of language use* in the data?

Looking at systems, and the options within them, is what this area of *Norms and Variations* is all about.

✦ ✦ ✦

✦ RESEARCH PATHWAYS ✦

Savoury snack names (British people eat more savoury snacks per head than Americans); names for shampoo, perfume, aftershave, and other cosmetic products, possibly contrasting 'green' products such as those in the Body Shop with more traditional versions, or contrasting those aimed at men with those aimed at women; the names of household cleaners from different eras, e.g. soap powders, toilet products, scouring powders/creams.

THE LANGUAGE OF OPTICIANS' SHOP NAMES

INITIAL ACTIVITY

Below is a collection of names of Opticians' shops. Read them through, and try to categorise these on the basis of the techniques being used. You may find the following headings useful as a starting point:

references to well-known idioms or sayings; use of homonyms (words that sound the same but have different spellings); use of numbers to replace words; words which suggest numerical order; polysemous words (where one word can have two different meanings)

First Sight	Look Right
Eye Openers	4 Sight
Second Vision	Vision Express
20/20 Vision	Eye Site
Eyes Right	4 Eyes
Spec Tackle	A Sight for Sore Eyes
Eyes Front	Eyeland
Eye 2 Eye	Spex
Eye Contact	Insight
Second Sight	New Look
Special Eyes	

When you have finished, try to think of some more possible names for Opticians' shops. Here are some ideas, to get you going:

Popular sayings: an eye for an eye; giving someone the eye; if looks could kill; looking daggers; an eye for the main chance; eyeing someone up

Particular words/meanings: spectacular; a spectacle; a vision; visionary; hindsight; a sighting

◆ ◆ ◆

FURTHER ACTIVITY

Pool your categories and discuss your findings, if you were working in a group situation. Whatever your chosen method of working, consider the following:

● Were you able to group the names to show systems of language use?

● Decide why the companies used the particular techniques they did. What were they trying to suggest about their products?

Also consider your ideas on new names, explaining what connotations you were trying to attach to them, either orally or in note form for your file.

◆ ◆ ◆

✦ RESEARCH PATHWAYS ✦

Names of other high street shops – hairdressers, general household shops (e.g. 'Just Wot U Need', 'The Fulmonte', 'Top of the Pots'), clothes shops, beauty parlours, etc.

THE LANGUAGE OF GREETINGS CARDS

INITIAL ACTIVITY

Look at the two birth cards below and on on p.97. Analyse the language used in the two cards, and how it differs on the basis of gender of target group.

Think about all the different levels of language at work in the cards.

- Graphological level (the card for the girl was pink, while the boy's card was blue)
- Phonological level
- Semantic level
- Grammatical level
- Discourse level

> Tiny fingers, tiny toes,
> Rosebud mouth and button nose,
> Dainty pinks and frilly clothes—
> Precious things she soon outgrows.
>
> The biggest eyes, a toothless grin,
> Downy hair and peach-soft skin—
> Wide awake or all tucked in,
> She steals the hearts
> of doting kin...

> A wee, small voice, a tiny tear,
> Coming through so loud and clear,
> A cuddly bundle sweet and dear
> Who grows more precious
> year by year!
>
> Congratulations

Tiny fingers,
tiny toes,
Rosebud mouth,
and button nose,
Overalls,
and boy-type clothes,
Adorable suits
he soon outgrows,
The biggest eyes,
a toothless grin,
Downy hair,
and peach-soft skin—
Wide awake
or all tucked in,
He steals the hearts
of doting kin...

A wee small voice,
a tiny tear,
Coming through
so loud and clear,
A bundle of boy
so cuddly and dear,
Who grows
more precious
year by year!

Congratulations!

Verses reprinted with permission © AGC, Inc.

✦ ✦ ✦

FURTHER ACTIVITY or

If you were working in a group situation, share your findings on how the cards differ from each other, according to the gender of the baby. If you were working alone, write up your notes as a summary, in essay form.

Whatever your chosen working method, also consider the following:

● What other variations might you find, according to the type of audience being greeted (e.g. age)?

● How is the language used in these cards typical of greetings cards in general? What are the 'norms', or commonly found features, of such cards?

✦ ✦ ✦

✦ RESEARCH PATHWAYS ✦

Research:

— the variations in techniques found in greetings cards, e.g. use of humour; use of verse; interplay between the cover and the message inside; use of different images;

variations in typeface/use of handwriting; formulaic expressions used for greetings; use of language involving particular connotations (e.g. archaic language, use of emotive terms);

— the range of events and messages we mark by the use of greetings cards. Do you have any idea whether other cultures mark the same types of events, or use the same sorts of technique in their cards?

THE LANGUAGE OF 'MILLS AND BOON' BOOK TITLES

INITIAL ACTIVITY

Look at the collection of 'Mills and Boon' book titles below. Can you find any patterns or systems in the data?

Try to categorise the titles according to their *semantic* content – what connotations link several of the titles together, as trying to create similar pictures?

Create your own headings for the categories you find.

Are there also common *grammatical* patterns in the data?

Rage	Secret Fire
Fever	Dark Tyrant
The Caged Tiger	Loving in the Lion's Den
Desire	Dangerous Moonlight
Snow Bride	Untamed
With All My Worldly Goods	Kiss of a Tyrant
Lord of the Land	Wildfire Encounter
Midnight Lover	The Fires of Heaven
Dear Villain	King of Culla
Burning Obsession	Bridal Path
Night of Possession	Always the Boss
Summer in France	The Girl from Nowhere
Greek Island Magic	Makebelieve Marriage
A Modern Girl	Pacific Aphrodite
Dangerous Demon	Savage Surrender
A Girl Bewitched	Dangerous Compulsion
Sweet Conquest	Dear Demon

◆ ◆ ◆

FURTHER ACTIVITY

Share your ideas on the categories you have found, if you were working in a group situation. Whatever your chosen working method, consider the following:

● What do the various connotations and structures of the titles tell you about the world of 'Mills and Boon' books?

✦✦✦

✦ RESEARCH PATHWAYS ✦

Norms and variations in book 'blurbs'; authors' names; names of heroes and heroines.

THE LANGUAGE OF GRAVESTONES

INITIAL ACTIVITY

Below is a list of headings, epitaphs and verses offered by a funeral director to help relatives to choose an inscription for a grave.

Read them through, and look for patterns in language use:

Semantics: Are there particular ideas that occur frequently?
What metaphorical uses of language are evident in the data?
What are the connotations of the words and phrases used?

Grammar: Why are there particular grammatical structures in the data that are not in everyday use?
What structural patterning is evident within some of the phrases?
Why is it used?

Phonology: What aspects of sound patterning are evident, and why are they used?

Discourse: What do your observations suggest about our attitudes to death? For example, what is the function of gravestones and the language we choose to write on them?
Who is the language written by, and who is it aimed at?
Why do we choose certain forms of language and not others?

HEADINGS

Cherished Memories of . . .

Precious Are the Memories of . . .

Our Lady of Lourdes Pray for the Soul of . . .

Treasured Memories of . . .

The Saviour Has My Treasure . . .

In Loving Memory of . . .

EPITAPHS

IN GOD'S KEEPING

THE SAVIOUR HAS MY TREASURE

IN HEAVENLY LOVE ABIDING

THE LORD MADE A GAIN, WE A GREAT LOSS

PEACE, PERFECT PEACE

FOREVER IN OUR THOUGHTS

FOREVER IN OUR HEARTS

LOVING YOU ALWAYS, FORGETTING YOU NEVER.

PRECIOUS MEMORIES LEFT BEHIND

HE WHO DWELLETH IN LOVE, DWELLETH IN GOD

REST AFTER WEARINESS, PEACE AFTER PAIN

LOVES LAST GIFT; REMEMBRANCE

A BEAUTIFUL MEMORY LEFT BEHIND

SO DEARLY LOVED - SO SADLY MISSED

GOD'S FINGER TOUCHED HIM AND HE SLEPT

ANOTHER FLOWER FOR GOD'S GARDEN

SWEET ARE THE MEMORIES THAT NEVER FADE

RESTING WHERE NO SHADOWS FALL

IN OUR HEARTS HE WILL LIVE FOREVER

GONE FROM OUR HOME BUT NOT FROM OUR HEARTS

TO LIVE IN THE HEARTS OF THOSE WE LOVE -
                              IS NOT TO DIE

VERSES

Nothing is more precious
Than the thoughts we have of you,
To us you were so special
God must have thought so too.

There's a place in my heart called memory lane,
And in it dear . . . you will always remain.

Beautiful memories treasured forever
Of the golden days when we were together.

A tiny flower, lent not given
To bud on earth and bloom in heaven.

No one heard the footsteps
Of an angel drawing near,
As they took from earth to heaven
One we loved so dear.

Beautiful memories dearer than gold,
Of our loved one whose worth
Can never be told.

Memories are golden, we know that is true,
But we don't want memories we just want you.

A golden heart stopped beating,
Hard working hands laid to rest,
God broke our hearts to prove to us
He only takes the best.

◆ ◆ ◆

FURTHER ACTIVITY or

If you were working in a group situation, pool your ideas on the language use on gravestones. Are there patterns of language use to be observed?

If you were working alone, write up your notes into a summary, in essay form. Consider whether you could tabulate any of your findings, for purposes of economy.

Whatever your chosen working method, consider the following:

● What are your conclusions about public attitudes to death, and the function of graves and gravestone language?

◆ ◆ ◆

✦ RESEARCH PATHWAYS ✦

Language use in newspaper obituaries; variations in gravestone inscriptions according to gender; analysis of the euphemisms (and dysphemisms – 'impolite' language) used about death; historical changes in the language on gravestones.

2. Accent and Dialect

This area is concerned with the way in which language varies on a regional basis.

Accent refers to the sounds that are made by speakers; *dialect* refers to the words, grammatical structures and sayings that speakers have as part of their regional variety of language.

There is one accent, and one dialect, that are no longer regional varieties.

The accent called *Received Pronunciation*, while recognisable as originally a southern variety of speech, no longer marks someone as coming from a certain region. It now denotes someone as belonging to a middle class social group, and is often the accent heard on national news broadcasts.

The dialect called *Standard English*, which originally came from an area between the Midlands and London, is now an agreed common standard language taught in schools and used in written material which is designed to be understood in all areas of the country. Standard English can be spoken with any regional accent.

In studies of accent and dialect, regional varieties are often compared with RP and Standard English as benchmarks against which to measure regional forms. This should not suggest that RP and Standard English are better forms of language than regional varieties – although the belief that this is so is an idea that itself can be explored in language research.

INITIAL ACTIVITY

Look at the data on p.104, which is a phonemic transcription of an Aberdeen speaker's spontaneous speech.

Read it back to yourselves, deciding how the various words were spoken. You may need to refer to the phonemic alphabet which is given in *Section A, Unit 3, Decoding Spoken Texts* (p.45).

Then make a list of those words which are pronounced differently from how an RP speaker would say them.

Remember that there are some features of connected speech which all speakers will exhibit – if you need to refresh your memories on this, look back to the section mentioned above, and make a list of the features to look for. Separate the ordinary features of connected speech from those uses of sound that are characteristic of the regional accent.

Finally, when you have your list of words, try to trace a pattern of sound usage in the Aberdeen speaker's language; for example, does a particular sound occur several times in the same context?

The speaker is a 40 year-old woman reminiscing about her school days.

In this extract, she is talking about how she did in a Geography test, and comparing herself with her schoolfriend, Barbara.

Whole extract: I got three and she got two . . . out of fifty. I . . . that is absolutely . . . and we were second last . . . second bottom and bottom in the class, and that is, that is true, it . . . it is. I wasn't a dunce . . . I was a rebel . . . I wasn't a dunce. Um, Barbara was more clever than me, I mean, like I say, she was . . . she went into commercial . . . or she could've gone into commercial, but she didn't.

I	got	three	and	she	got
aɪ	gɒʔ	θri	ən	ʃi	gɒʔ
two	out	of	fifty	I	that
tu	aʊʔ	ə	fɪftɪ	aɪ	ðaʔ
is	absolutely	and	we	were	second
ɪz	absəlutlɪ	ən	wi	wɜɾ	sɛəkən
last	second	bottom	and	bottom	in	the
lasʈ	sɛəkən	bɔʔəm	əm	bɔʔəm	ən	ðə
class	and	that	is	that	is	true
klas	ən	ðaʔ	ɪz	ðaʔ	ɪz	tru
it	it	is	I	wasn't	a	dunce
ɪʔ	ɪʔ	ɪz	aɪ	wɔzn	ə	dʌns
I	was	a	rebel	I	wasn't
æ	wəz	ə	rɛəbal	æ	wɔzn
a	dunce	um	Barbara	was	more
ə	dʌns	em	bærbræ	wəz	mɔɾ
clever	than	me	I	mean	like	I
klɛəvəɾ	ðan	mi	ə	min	laɪk	ə
say	she	was	she	went	into
sɛɪ	ʃi	wəz	ʃi	wɛnʈ	ɪnʈə
commercial	or	she	could've	gone
kəmɛəʃəl	ɔr	ʃi	kʊdə	gɒn
into	commercial	but	she	didn't
ɪnʈə	kəmɛəʃəl	bʌʔ	ʃi	dɪdnə

◆ ◆ ◆

FURTHER ACTIVITY I or

Share your findings, if you were working in a group situation. Were you able to identify some patterns of sound which systematically differ from RP pronunciations?

If you were working alone, try to express your findings economically, by expressing them in tabulated form, or as a set of 'rules'.

Whatever your chosen method of working, consider the following:

● Can you see that, although the speaker is using features of regional accent, she is speaking throughout in Standard English?

◆ ◆ ◆

FURTHER ACTIVITY II

Read through the interview below, between a researcher (R) and a retired proprietor (P) of a small shop.

Try to identify some regional dialect features – vocabulary and grammatical structures – that differ from Standard English.

R: how did you keep your tick records
P: put it in a book
R: you haven't kept that book
P: no/I've had some good debts I've had some bad uns and I've had/I think about three years after I'd sold shop/I sold to a man what worked with me at tannery and he still kept on working/and I said to him how's business Bill/he said not so bad he said but you've some bloody bad payers haven't you/I said well no I haven't but that/that has gone out of existence/you see/we lived in Reservoir Street and there wasn't a shop in the district where they would let us have credit/in finish I'd got to go over to me Uncle Jim's in Dean Road on him to get us some bread butter cheese or anything
R: but quite a few people who came into your shop you let them have
P: oh yes yes/which was never very never very great/you'd get these as want cigarettes/want a pack of cigarettes
R: did they settle up with you at the end of the week or did they let it go on for longer than that
P: no the biggest majority settled at the end of the week/now they had trouble the next door where the mixed was/where they had the tea coffee sugar bacon butter cheese
R: why should they have more trouble than you
P: because theirs was eatables/the biggest majority was eatables/especially for the family where in those days they had/if you hadn't a family of four or five there was something wrong in that family/so/anyway/I told you we lived in Channing Street and there were/were it fourteen houses or is there sixteen houses on either side/only/one person was ill in that street/the remainder went in some time or another to see how she was going on/and if a baby was born/they were running in with basins of gruel/you know for years I never drank tea out of a cup or a pint pot/always had it in a basin/oh it's lovely out of a basin
R: tastes better does it
P: I'll tell thee/you'd go in and it was a common thing to see/the door wide open and about half-a-dozen home-made flour cakes stood up against the skirting board cooling off/where they did their own/where mother did her own baking
R: why would they cool them there/why
P: because it were cheaper/it was a common thing to see them coming back with a dozen of flour on their head and they were knocking it together/and/it was cheaper/they saved by baking their own/and I reckon in seven houses out of ten you would see on the table a stone jar containing black/treacle or syrup/syrup/treacle/or black treacle

Source: Manchester Metropolitan University Oral History Unit

◆ ◆ ◆

FURTHER ACTIVITY III

If you were working in a group situation, share your findings on the interviewee's regional dialect features. If you were working alone, write a summary for your file of the main patterns of usage you found. Whatever your chosen working method, consider the following:

● It is a well recorded fact that dialect vocabulary has been dying out for a long time, while accent and some aspects of regional grammar remain strong. Why do you think that is?

◆ ◆ ◆

FURTHER ACTIVITY IV

The student who researched the accent of the Aberdeen area also collected some Aberdeen dialect vocabulary and grammar by questionnaire method.

Consulting secondary source material, she offered a number of informants of different ages, sexes, and occupations the words in the column on the left, and asked them for a translation. Their answers were as follows:

```
clipe = a tell-tale (or to tell tales)
quine = a girl
loon = a boy
cowpe = overturn, turn over, fall over, make a mess
greetin' = crying, weeping
blake = shoe/boot polish
stottin' = drunk, bouncing (a ball)
yurded = clarted(!), dirty, filthy
sappy dubs = mud, wet mud
cloot = cloth
humming = smelly, stinking
plooky = spotty, pimply
scunnered = fed up, sick of, been tricked
```

These terms were offered to informants as a stimulus to memory; they were then asked to volunteer some expressions of their own which they considered part of the Aberdeen dialect. Some of these expressions were as follows:

```
fit like = how are you?
fit a day afa wither = what a day – awful weather!
fits this fur any wi? = what's this for anyway?
fit are ye deeing? = what are you doing?
fa? = who?
far i' yi gan? = where are you going?
muckle = much                          stravaig = to stroll
bairns, geets = children               howk = dig out
```

simmet = vest	sair heid = sore head
starvin' = cold	redd = set in order
ging = go	chanty = toilet, chamber pot
hoose = house	skink, hough = shin of beef
wifie = woman	rake = to roam
al = old	kirk = church
puggled, peched = tired	brig = bridge
glaiket = silly, a show-off	gleg = sharp, quick
wee = little	hippen = nappy
canny = careful	the streen = last night
dinna = don't	ken = know
canna = can't	breeks = trousers
grumph = a moaner	sark = shirt
div = do	crabbit = bad tempered
feart = frightened	neeps = turnips
scaffie = person who sweeps rubbish	tatties = potatoes
bonny = good looking	bampot = fool
orra = odd, left over	gan hame = going home

Now try to answer the following:

● The boundary between what we call 'accent' and what we call 'dialect' is not always clear-cut, because sometimes you could classify a term or phrase as either a variation of pronunciation, or an entirely separate and different vocabulary item. Look at the list, and decide whether there are any terms you would call 'accent variation' rather than 'dialect vocabulary'.

● Which of the terms on the list would be known by many English speakers – even though they may not use them – and which would be entirely foreign? How do you think English speakers might have learnt some of the terms?

● Which examples would you call dialect vocabulary, and which dialect grammar?

● Try to group together the different terms as far as possible, according to the areas they describe or name. Are there dialect terms in the regional language of your own area or family which cover similar areas? Try to think of some equivalents.

● In the survey, many more examples were offered by older speakers than younger ones, and many more by working-class speakers than middle-class ones. However, everyone listed one or more of the first six phrases. How would you account for these results?

◆ ◆ ◆

FURTHER ACTIVITY V

Share your conclusions on the questions outlined above, if you were working in a group situation. Whatever your chosen working method, do the following:

- Tabulate any examples you have of dialect terms of your own area
  (For a list of common regional dialect grammar variations, see A. Goddard, J. Keen and J. Shuttleworth, *English Language 'A' Level: The Starter Pack* (Framework Press, 1991))

- Consider the methods of data collection used by researchers in this unit. What are the strengths and weaknesses of each? Would it be valid to use a range of different methods in one research project?

✦ RESEARCH PATHWAYS ✦

Comparison between a regional accent and RP; comparison between a regional dialect and Standard English; exploration of the accent/dialect variations of one speaker in different situations; analysis of attitudes to accent variety (informants responding to differently accented speakers); analysis of accent use in TV advertisements; representations of accent and dialect in written material.

3. Stylistics

Stylistics is concerned with style choices in language.

Style is a rather wide and all-encompassing term which is often used rather loosely. In Linguistics, it refers, like the term 'discourse', to the way in which whole texts – spoken and written – work, on a number of different levels, to create an overall impression or message.

Stylistic analysis always asks two main questions:

- How is the text put together – how does it work? This may well involve consideration of how the text is distinctive: in other words, what makes it what it is?

- What are the effects of language use in the text – what is the text trying to do?

There is a virtually limitless list of texts which could be explored.

The following are just some which researchers have found interesting to analyse: *Examples*: literature; newspapers; magazines; comics; advertisements; TV programmes; non-fiction school textbooks; particular genres of speech.

Stylistic analysis is much easier to attempt if you set up a comparison between different texts in the area you want to research. This is by no means the only way to approach stylistics, but it can be useful because language choices are easier to spot if you can contrast them with alternatives.

Literature

Literature is interesting to research because it is a very self-conscious and deliberate form of language use which aims to create specific effects.

Some forms of literature can be problematic, however, because they are too large and unwieldy to form the basis of a small and well-focused piece of language research. This is particularly true of prose fiction in the form of lengthy whole novels. What is needed, then, is careful consideration of the types of question that can be answered by looking at particular sections or extracts. This is the issue addressed by the activities in this unit.

INITIAL ACTIVITY

Read the two extracts that follow. Both are from *Jane Eyre*, by Charlotte Brontë. *Extract A* is from the original text, published in 1848; *extract B* is an abridged version of the same part of the story, designed for adult slow readers and published by Kennett books in the 1950s.

Two possible questions that could be asked about these texts are the following:

- What has been left out of the Kennett version, and why?

- How has the language used in the extracts changed over the course of time?

It would be possible in one project to ask both questions, as they are interrelated: modern editors would be anxious to avoid language that was archaic, in their attempt to simplify the abridged version.

Take each question in turn, and make some notes in preparation for feedback to the whole group, or for your own file.

EXTRACT A

I HAD forgotten to draw my curtain, which I usually did; and also to let down my window-blind. The consequence was that when the moon, which was full and bright (for the night was fine), came in her course to that space in the sky opposite my casement, and looked in at me through the unveiled panes, her glorious gaze roused me. Awaking in the dead of night, I opened my eyes on her disc – silver-white and crystal clear. It was beautiful, but too solemn: I half rose, and stretched my arm to draw the curtain.

Good God! What a cry!

The night – its silence – its rest, was rent in twain by a savage, a sharp, a shrilly sound, that ran from end to end of Thornfield Hall.

My pulse stopped; my heart stood still; my stretched arm was paralyzed. The cry died, and was not renewed. Indeed, whatever being uttered that fearful shriek could not soon repeat it: not the widest-winged condor on the Andes could, twice in succession, send out such a yell from the cloud shrouding his eyrie. The thing delivering such utterance must rest ere it could repeat the effort.

It came out of the third storey; for it passed overhead. And overhead – yes, in the room just above my chamber ceiling – I now heard a struggle: a deadly one it seemed from the noise; and a half smothered voice shouted –

"Help! help! help!" three times rapidly.

"Will no one come?" it cried; and then, while the staggering and stamping went on wildly, I distinguished, through plank and plaster:—

"Rochester! Rochester! for God's sake, come!"

A chamber-door opened: some one ran, or rushed, along the gallery. Another step stamped on the flooring above, and something fell; and there was silence.

I had put on some clothes, though horror shook all my limbs. I issued from my apartment. The sleepers were all around: ejaculations, terrified murmurs, sounded in every room; door after door unclosed; one looked out, and another looked out; the gallery filled. Gentlemen and ladies alike had quitted their beds; and "Oh! what is it?" – "Who is hurt?" – "What has happened?" – "Fetch a light!" – "Is it fire?" – "Are there robbers?" – "Where shall we run?" was demanded confusedly on all hands. But for the moonlight they would have been in complete darkness. They ran to and fro; they crowded together, some sobbed, some stumbled: the confusion was inextricable.

"Where the devil is Rochester?" cried Colonel Dent. "I cannot find him in his bed."

"Here! here!" was shouted in return. "Be composed, all of you. I am coming."

And the door at the end of the gallery opened, and Mr Rochester advanced with a candle: he had just descended from the upper storey. One of the ladies ran to him directly: she seized his arm: it was Miss Ingram.

"What awful event has taken place?" said she. "Speak! let us know the worst at once!"

"But don't pull me down or strangle me," he replied: for the Misses Eshton were clinging about him now; and the two dowagers, in vast white wrappers, were bearing down on him like ships in full sail.

"All's right! – all's right!" he cried. "It's a mere rehearsal of 'Much Ado about Nothing'. Ladies, keep off; or I shall wax dangerous."

And dangerous he looked; his black eyes darted sparks. Calming himself by an effort, he added—

"A servant has had the nightmare; that is all. She's an excitable, nervous person: she construed her dream into an apparition, or something of that sort, no doubt; and has taken a fit with fright. Now, then, I must see you all back into your rooms; for, till the house is settled, she cannot be looked after. Gentlemen, have the goodness to set the ladies the example. Miss Ingram, I am sure you will not fail in evincing superiority to idle terrors. Amy and Louisa, return to your nests like a pair of doves, as you are. Mesdames" (to the dowagers), "you will take cold to a dead certainty, if you stay in this chill gallery any longer."

EXTRACT B

I had forgotten to draw my curtain, and when the moon rose, full and bright, its light roused me from sleep. Awaking in the dead of night I opened my eyes on her silver-white disc. I half rose and stretched my arm to draw the curtain.

Heavens! What a cry!

The silence of the night was ripped apart by a fearful shriek. It ran from end to end of Thornfield Hall. My heart stood still; my stretched arm froze. The cry died, and sounded no more.

It had come out of the third storey. And now, overhead – yes, in the room just above my own – I heard the sounds of a struggle: a deadly one it seemed from the noise. A half-smothered voice shouted: "Help! help! help!" three times rapidly. And then: "Rochester! For God's sake, come!"

I heard a door open. Someone rushed along the gallery. Another step stamped on the flooring above and something fell; and there was silence.

I pulled on some clothes, though horror shook all my limbs. Everyone, it seemed, was awake. I went out into the gallery. Door after door opened. The gallery filled with ladies and gentlemen. "What is it?" – "What has happened?" – "Are there robbers?" – "Where shall we run?" was asked on every side.

"Where the devil is Rochester?" cried Colonel Dent. "I can't find him in his bed."

"Here! Here!" came a shout. "Calm yourselves! I'm coming now!"

The door at the end of the gallery opened. Mr. Rochester appeared with a candle.

"It's all right!" he cried, and his black eyes darted sparks in the candlelight. "A servant has had a nightmare, that is all. She's an excitable person, and has taken a fit with fright. Now then, I must see you all back into your rooms, for, till the house is settled, she cannot be looked after."

◆ ◆ ◆

FURTHER ACTIVITY I ŧ or ⊕

Feed your results back to the whole group, if you have been working in a group situation. If you have been working individually, write up your file notes using the following headings:

- What are the main omissions from the Kennett text, and why do you think the editors chose to abridge the text in this way?

- What aspects of language change are noticeable when the two texts are compared? In particular, are there specific words and phrases used in the original text that have died out or changed their meanings?

- Are there features in the original that may have been changed *either* to simplify *or* to modernise, and it is difficult to say which motive the editors had? Can you identify some examples of style that could be in either category?

It is important to realise that you do not need to have neat and tidy answers: the fact that you are able to speculate on the above questions is what language research projects are all about.

◆ ◆ ◆

FURTHER ACTIVITY II ŧ or ŧ ŧ ŧ

The text that follows is a whole short story, written by Virginia Woolf.

Its title suggests that it is a story written within a particular genre.

Before you start to read the story, brainstorm the ingredients you would expect to have in a story in that genre.

When you have finished, read through the story, and consider how far your expectations have been met: is Virginia Woolf following the genre, or is she playing with the reader's expectations?

A HAUNTED HOUSE

Whatever hour you woke there was a door shutting. From room to room they went, hand in hand, lifting here, opening there, making sure – a ghostly couple.

'Here we left it,' she said. And he added, 'Oh, but here too!' 'It's upstairs,' she murmured. 'And in the garden,' he whispered. 'Quietly,' they said, 'or we shall wake them.'

But it wasn't that you woke us. Oh, no. 'They're looking for it; they're drawing the curtain, one might say, and so read on a page or two. 'Now they've found it,' one would be certain, stopping the pencil on the margin. And then, tired of reading, one might rise and see for oneself, the house all empty, the doors standing open, only the wood pigeons bubbling with content and the hum of the threshing machine sounding from the farm. 'What did I come in here for? What did I want to find?' My hands were empty. 'Perhaps it's upstairs then?' The apples were in the loft. And so down again, the garden still as ever, only the book had slipped into the grass.

But they had found it in the drawing-room. Not that one could ever see them. The window panes reflected apples, reflected roses; all the leaves were green in the glass. If they moved in the drawing-room the apple only turned its yellow side. Yet, the moment after, if the door was opened, spread about the floor, hung upon the walls, pendant from the ceiling – what? My hands were empty. The shadow of a thrush crossed the carpet; from the deepest wells of silence the wood pigeon drew its bubble of sound. 'Safe, safe, safe,' the pulse of the house beat softly. 'The treasure buried; the room . . .' the pulse stopped short. Oh, was that the buried treasure?

A moment later the light had faded. Out in the garden then? But the trees spun darkness for a wandering beam of sun. So fine, so rare, coolly sunk beneath the surface the beam I sought always burnt behind the glass. Death was the glass; death was between us; coming to the woman first, hundreds of years ago, leaving the house, sealing all the windows; the rooms were darkened. He left it, left her, went North, went East, saw the stars turned into the Southern sky; sought the house, found it dropped beneath the Downs. 'Safe, safe, safe,' the pulse of the house beat gladly. 'The Treasure yours.'

The wind roars up the avenue. Trees stoop and bend this way and that. Moonbeams splash and spill wildly in the rain. But the beam of the lamp falls straight from the window. The candle burns stiff and still. Wandering through the house, opening the windows, whispering not to wake us, the ghostly couple seek their joy.

'Here we slept,' she says. And he adds, 'Kisses without number.' 'Waking in the morning –' 'Silver between the trees –' 'Upstairs –' 'In the garden –' 'When summer came –' 'In winter snowtime –' The doors go shutting far in the distance, gently knocking like the pulse of a heart.

Nearer they come; cease at the doorway. The wind falls, the rain slides silver down the glass. Our eyes darken; we hear no steps beside us; we see no lady spread her ghostly cloak. His hands shield the lantern. 'Look,' he breathes. 'Sound asleep. Love upon their lips.'

Stooping, holding their silver lamp above us, long they look and deeply. Long they pause. The wind drives straightly; the flame stoops slightly. Wild beams of moonlight cross both floor and wall, and, meeting, stain the faces bent; the faces pondering; the faces that search the sleepers and seek their hidden joy.

'Safe, safe, safe,' the heart of the house beats proudly. 'Long years –' he sighs. 'Again you found me.' 'Here,' she murmurs, 'sleeping; in the garden reading; laughing, rolling apples in the loft. Here we left our treasure –' Stooping, their light lifts the lids upon my eyes. 'Safe! safe! safe! the pulse of the house beats wildly. Waking, I cry 'Oh, is this your buried treasure? The light in the heart.'

When you have read the story and discussed how far Virginia Woolf has followed a well-known literary genre, there is another question that it's obvious to ask:

● Why is the story so confusing, and so difficult to make sense of?

We need to assume that Woolf was capable of writing clearly if she wanted to, so the answer can't be that she couldn't string a sentence together properly. So the confusion is deliberate. Why, then, did she write in this way, and how is the confusion created in the language? This could be the main question of a research project on this literary text. In order to answer these questions, think about the following:

● Why should the writer want to make the reader search for clarity and meaning in this text? Could that be part of the message of the story?

- How much confusion and deliberate suspense is created by:
  - the use of pronouns, referring to the various people in the story? This feature is called *reference* and is an aspect of *cohesion* in writing – in other words, the way the text 'hangs together';
  - unusual sentence structure, where important information is left right to the end?
  - sentences that have parts missing, e.g. objects, the thing or person having something done to it?
  - *agency* – whether people or inanimate things are carrying out actions?

The passage also has a rhythmic quality which contributes to its pace and cohesion without clarifying any meaning. This means that, even though the reader might not be able to make sense of the story, he/she feels that the text has shape, and structure. This encourages him/her to struggle to solve the puzzle of the test.

In order to understand this process, look at the following features of language:

- Repeated grammatical structures, and variations in sentence length

- Sound patterning – the text's *phonological* structure

✦ ✦ ✦

FURTHER ACTIVITY III

If you were working in a group situation, share the results of your discussions on the various aspects of Virginia Woolf's story. If you have been working individually, write up your notes, using the headings outlined above.

Whatever your chosen working methods, consider the following overall questions:

- Can you see how the writing is very self-consciously making the reader search for meaning?

- Why should the writer want the reader to search for meaning?

Short stories and writing in particular literary genres often yield interesting research questions: short story writers have to pay particular attention to shape and structure because of the constraints of space; writing in particular genres usually follows a recognisable pattern. Both these aspects are of course traceable in the language used.

✦ ✦ ✦

FURTHER ACTIVITY IV

On p.115 are three openings of stories: one is from a piece of autobiographical fiction; one is from a fairy story; and one is from a detective novel.

Decide which is which, and then decide how you worked out the answers: how does the language used in such openings set up expectations in readers that they are going to get a particular type of story?

A) Like most people I lived for a long time with my mother and father. My father liked to watch the wrestling, my mother liked to wrestle; it didn't matter what. She was in the white corner and that was that.

She hung out the largest sheets on the windiest days. She *wanted* the Mormons to knock on the door. At election time in a Labour mill town she put a picture of the Conservative candidate in the window.

She had never heard of mixed feelings. There were friends and there were enemies.

B) Once there was a girl whose boyfriend drowned in the sea. Her parents could do nothing to console her. Nor did any of the other suitors interest her – she wanted the fellow who drowned and no-one else. Finally she took a chunk of blubber and carved it into the shape of her drowned boyfriend. Then she carved the boyfriend's face. It was a perfect likeness.

'Oh, if only he were real!' she thought.

She rubbed the blubber against her genitals, round and round, and suddenly it came alive.

C) I had forgotten the smell. Even with the South Works on strike and Wisconsin Steel padlocked and rusting away, a pungent mix of chemicals streamed in through the engine vents. I turned off the car heater, but the stench – you couldn't call it air – slid through minute cracks in the Chevy's windows, burning my eyes and sinuses.

I followed Route 41 south. A couple of miles back it had been Lake Shore Drive, with Lake Michigan spewing foam against the rocks on the left, expensive high rises haughtily looking on from the right. At Seventy-ninth Street, the lake disappeared abruptly.

◆ ◆ ◆

FURTHER ACTIVITY V  **or**

If you have been working in groups, share your results and discussions with the other groups. (Answers as on p.116, if you need them). Whatever your chosen working method, consider the following:

● How did you work out which was which; how was the language of each characteristic of a particular genre of writing?

● What is the function of an opening of a story?

● What aspects are often covered in the way a novel or short story opens?

◆ ◆ ◆

FURTHER ACTIVITY VI **or**

You could probably debate for some time the issue of what genre of writing the Bible represents – is it fiction or non-fiction, for example? Is it a recipe for good behaviour, or an instruction manual? Whatever the answers to these questions, it is often fruitful data for research purposes because so many different versions of it exist.

On p.116 are two different versions of the 'Lord is My Shepherd' Psalm.

Analyse how they differ stylistically: what are the differences in the language used, and what effects do these differences create?

KING JAMES 1611

The Lord is my shepherd; I shall not want.

He maketh me to lie down in green pastures; he leadeth me beside the still waters.

He restoreth my soul; he leadeth me in the paths of righteousness for his name's sake.

Yea, though I walk through the valley of the shadow of death, I will fear no evil: for thou art with me; thy rod and thy staff they comfort me.

Thou preparest a table before me in the presence of mine enemies: thou anointest my head with oil; my cup runneth over.

Surely goodness and mercy shall follow me all the days of my life; and I will dwell in the house of the Lord forever.

YORKSHIRE DIALECT 1922

T'owd boss luks after mi, ah want for nowt.
'e sees as 'ow there's fields weer ah c'n sit missen dahn,
or tek a walk alongside o't' dams.

Bigod, ah feels missen agen,
's reight, t'foller 'im, 'cos e's t'Boss.

Aye, tho't' valley's thick wi' smooak,
   an' Death's in it, ah'll fear nowt,
for th'art wi' mi, th'art mi backbooan an' mi
   walking-stick; the keeps mi snug.

The ses: Sit thi dahn an' eeat;
   ne'er mind as theer's them as grudge thee it,

Tha smooths mi 'air, an' fills brimful mi mug.

F'shooa thi blessin' 'n compassion

   'll be wi' mi till smooak clears
   an' ah'm wi' thee
   in t'ouse that's allus, allus thine.

Answers (Further Activity IV p.114)

A) Autobiography – Jeanette Winterson, *Oranges Are Not the Only Fruit* (Pandora, 1986)

B) Fairy Tale – 'Blubber Boy' in Angela Carter (ed.), *The Virago Book of Fairy Tales* (Virago, 1991)

C) Detective Novel – Sara Paretsky, *Toxic Shock* (Penguin, 1988)

FURTHER ACTIVITY VII or

If you have been working in groups, pool your ideas on the different versions of the Psalm: how do they differ in their language use? what are the effects of each text? why are the texts different?

Whatever your chosen working methods, create some headings which would be useful to have as the basis for an analysis on these texts, then write up your notes under these headings.

✦ RESEARCH PATHWAYS ✦

Differences between literary representations of speech, and real speech; descriptions of the same type of event in different pieces of literature, e.g. sexual encounters; analysis of fictive languages, e.g. in *1984* by George Orwell and *Riddley Walker* by Russell Hoban; male and female poets' treatment of the same theme; bias and techniques used in literature written for children; literature in translation compared with the original foreign language text; particular linguistic techniques used by an individual writer, e.g. Caryl Churchill, Harold Pinter.

Newspapers

Just as there is no one 'language of literature', so there is no such thing as 'the language of newspapers': although there are certain features which readers expect to see when they open their daily papers – such as photographs with explanatory captions, headlines, articles written in columns, and so on – the writers of news features choose language to construct the meanings that they want to convey on particular topics at particular times. So although it is possible to make some observations about certain conventions of language use in newspapers, there is no one language that they all follow.

Sometimes, contrasts are drawn between papers on the basis of their size, or on the basis of exclusiveness versus popular appeal; the larger 'broadsheets' such as *The Guardian* and *The Times*, which have relatively small circulation figures, are sometimes termed 'quality' papers, and are compared with the smaller, more popular 'tabloids' such as *The Sun* or *The Mirror*. Such contrasts obscure a wide range of differences; for example, *The Sun* and *The Mirror* are polar opposites politically, as are *The Guardian* and *The Times*. The political affiliation of any newspaper is by far the strongest influence on what is reported in its pages, and how news is portrayed. All news reportage is mediated by the belief system of its management and editorial line, so there is arguably no such thing as 'the absolute truth': the idea, therefore, that 'quality' papers tell the truth while 'popular' papers perpetrate lies is, in itself, an example of bias.

Confused ideas about the social class of a paper's readership and about readers' 'intelligence' and reading ability also befuddle the analysis of newspaper language. Often, assumptions are made about these issues from the start, then the research becomes an attempt to make any 'findings' fall into line with what has already been decided: this is the opposite of research, since real research is an open-minded exploration with no narrow preconceptions about results.

So how can anything useful be discovered about language use in newspapers? The starting point must be the language itself, and how it is used: all speculations about the implications of the language use need to come afterwards.

If you want to compare the treatment of a particular story in different newspapers, you need to choose newspapers whose political affiliations are different. An example of such a contrast would be *The Sun*, which is right-wing, and *The Guardian*, which is relatively left-wing. One difficulty in attempting to find a common story is that different newspapers tend to cover different topics. The exception to this is when a very big story breaks, which all papers will want to cover. However, since this is likely to be a major catastrophe of some kind – such as an earthquake, train crash, or ferry disaster – it is probable that all papers will treat the subject in a fairly dramatic way. News coverage in any one paper may extend to several pages, which then presents the problem of selection. It is better, therefore, to try to find a common story where the papers' different political stances are likely to come to the fore in the language chosen to describe it.

INITIAL ACTIVITY

Read through the two different versions of the same story on pp.119–120.

The story concerns the break out, several years ago, of a number of inmates from the Maze prison in Northern Ireland.

The issue of political terrorism is one which the papers are likely to have very different ideas about.

Extract A is from *The Guardian*; *extract B* is from *The Sun*.

Read the articles through once, in order to gain an overall impression of their general approach. Then compare the articles on a range of different language levels. Here is a reminder of what they are, and some examples of what to look at in each level:

Graphological level: The layout, images, typeface, etc. and their effects

Phonological level: Whether the language used involves any sound patterning, and, if so, why

Semantic level: The choice of words and phrases, and their connotations; the subject matter, and how it is organised

Grammatical level: Use of active/passive constructions, use of repeated structures, sentence length and type, connectives used

Discourse level: Viewpoint constructed by the whole text, and its desired effect on the reader

EXTRACT A

27 Maze escapers still free

Gaol break checkpoint: Armed troops stopping cars at a roadblock after the escape from the Maze

From Bob Rodwell in Belfast

Twenty-seven IRA prisoners were being hunted last night after 38 broke out of the Maze Prison, near Belfast. One prison officer was fatally stabbed and six were wounded during the escape.

One prison officer was believed to be in a critical condition with gunshot wounds to the head, and at least one recaptured prisoner was in hospital. The nature of his injuries and his condition were not known, but according to one report he was shot when he refused to surrender.

Late last night army helicopters carrying powerful searchlights flew over the countryside around the prison, but most of the escapers were thought to have covered substantial distances before the full cordon of road blocks was in place.

According to a spokesman for the Northern Ireland Office the prisoners, from a segregated Republican block, produced firearms and knives, and overpowered the staff, taking some of the prison officers' uniforms and putting them on.

When a food lorry arrived from the prison kitchens it was stolen and the prisoners drove to the main gate of the prison, where they again produced firearms and knives.

A quick-thinking prison officer blocked the gate with his own car and the prisoners made off on foot after a scuffle during which the fatal stabbing happened and shots were fired. Police said that there were scenes of "total bedlam" as the prisoners scattered around the roads surrounding the gaol, which is eight miles south-west of Belfast.

Cars were hijacked and according to reports up to ten prisoners escaped in one vehicle. Several of those recaptured were seized on Ulster's M1 motorway, which runs along the southern side of the prison. The escapers broke up into several parties and one group was seen to make for the banks of the nearby river Lagan, where they were seen to change from their civilian-style prison clothing into genuine civvies which were apparently hidden for them in plastic bags on the river bank. Some reports spoke of prisoners dressed only in their underpants when they broke out.

Four of the men recaptured were caught as they swam across the Lagan.

Last night road blocks were in place around a wide radius from the prison and a man-hunt, employing thousands of police and soldiers was under way.

The escapers came from cells in a section of the gaol, which contains the H blocks where 10 Republican hunger strikers fasted to death in 1981.

A search of Block H7 after the break-out found 20 rounds of ammunition.

One woman, who was out walking past the Maze at the time of the escape, said: "There were men running around the fields. After about half an hour I saw a policeman holding a gun and shouting to prisoners to halt. One was taken back to the gates and then three more. They were marched down the road and held against a wall."

One escaper was chased by a soldier near the prison. After pursuing him for a short distance the soldier fired a single shot, at which the man stopped and surrendered.

As he was led back to the prison by his captor he called out to bystanders, "Oh well, it was worth a try."

Mr James Prior, the Northern Ireland Secretary, was duty minister at Stormont over the weekend. Last night he ordered an "immediate and searching inquiry at the highest level into all aspects of the escape."

The Northern Ireland Office said that Mr Prior had satisfied himself that all the necessary resources of the security forces had been and would be deployed in order to recapture the escaped prisoners.

The reference by the Northern Ireland Office to a "segregated Republican block" is the first official admission that segregation of prisoners, strongly demanded by many Loyalist politicians, has been reintroduced in Northern Irelands prisons.

Until now the official line has been that all prisoners would be treated equally as common criminals and that segregation would not be introduced.

The escape will certainly be hailed by many in the Provisional IRA as a major feat and will do much to restore its morale and that of the Irish National Liberation Army after the reverses they have suffered in recent months particularly from the effects of the "supergrass" trials.

The escape may cloud the political future of the Northern Ireland Office Minister of State, Mr Nicholas Scott.

After the general election he had extra responsibility placed on him, including the control of Ulster's prisons.

Mr Colin Steel, the chairman of the Prison Officers' Association in England and Wales, said last night that he had been in close touch with the POA in Northern Ireland. He was "extremely concerned" that

Turn to back page, col. 7

First published in *The Guardian* (Bob Rodwell)

EXTRACT B

PRISON GUARD KILLED
50 IRA men flee

By MIKE FIELDER, TONY SNOW and TREVOR HANNA

A GUARD was killed as up to 50 IRA terrorists shot their way to freedom from Belfast's Maze Prison yesterday.

The officer was stabbed in bloody running battles with the dangermen. A second guard was shot in the head and seriously wounded in the breakout — the biggest ever in Britain.

As the fugitives hit the streets they dragged motorists from passing cars and sped off in their hijacked vehicles.

Last night 16 of the prisoners had been rounded up as Ulster security forces mounted a massive hunt.

The prisoners escaped by hijacking a fruit lorry when it arrived from the prison kitchen at their block. They produced handguns and overpowered the driver and prison officers with him.

SHOTS

Then, in uniforms they had taken from the guards, they drove the fruit lorry to the prison main gate, where they confronted guards with guns and knives.

One officer blocked the exit with his car but the prisoners escaped on foot.

Several shots are believed to have been fired

THE HUNT IS ON: Soldiers check cars at a roadblock

First published in *The Sun* (Mike Fielder, Tony Snow and Trevor Hanna)

♦ ♦ ♦

FURTHER ACTIVITY I

If you have been working in groups, share your ideas on the language used in the two newspaper articles. Whatever your chosen method of working, consider the following:

● From the evidence in the language, what would you say were the main differences between the two papers in their attitudes to the event they are describing?

● What assumptions are the papers making about what their readers are interested in?

◆ ◆ ◆

FURTHER ACTIVITY II

Another useful approach to the study of language use in newspapers is to take a historical perspective, and trace the treatment of a particular subject over the course of time in specific papers.

Below is a range of headlines all concerned with royal births, taken from *The Times* and *The Daily Mirror* in 1948 (the birth of Prince Charles) and 1982 (the birth of Prince William).

Decide whether, in your opinion, any changes have taken place in the way the two papers headlined the royal births.

Where changes have taken place, how would you describe the differences in language use, and how would you account for them?

THE TIMES

	1948	1982
Day 1 Page 1	A SON FOR THE PRINCESS	A SON FOR PRINCESS: 7LB BABY AND MOTHER DOING WELL
Page 2	CHEERING CROWDS AT BUCKINGHAM PALACE	CROWD MOBS NEW FATHER OUTSIDE HOSPITAL
Day 2 Page 1	WIDE REJOICING AT BIRTH OF THE PRINCE CONGRATULATIONS FROM ALL PARTS OF THE WORLD	CHEERS HAIL THE DEBUT OF A SLEEPING PRINCE

THE DAILY MIRROR

	1948	1982
Day 1 Page 1 Page 2	AN 8LB BOY: BOTH DOING WELL	THAT'S OUR BOY NICE ONE CHARLIE . . . NICE ONE SON
Day 2 Page 1	THE BABY HAS ELIZABETH'S FACE, HAIR LIKE PHILIP	FATHER'S PRIDE

When you have finished, go on to the activity on p.122.

FURTHER ACTIVITY III

Now look at the four articles on pp.123–125, from the *Sheffield Morning Telegraph*. All the articles are concerned with royal weddings, and, more specifically, about two aspects of the ceremonies:

● The popular reaction of the crowds in London to the marriage celebrations of Lady Elizabeth Bowes-Lyon (the Queen Mother) to the then Duke of York (*Article A*: 1923) and Prince Charles to Lady Diana Spencer (*Article B*: 1981)

● Plans for the respective royal honeymoons (*Articles C* and *D*; 1923 and 1981, respectively)

Decide how far the language use in the paper has changed over the years, and which aspects of language are the main source of change.

Why do you think changes have taken place in the paper's reportage?

FURTHER ACTIVITY IV

If you have been working in groups, share your ideas on the differences between the various pieces of language data you have been analysing.

Whatever your chosen working method, create some headings for analysis which would be useful to base an analysis on, and write up your findings under these headings.

Also consider the usefulness of the types of contrast you have been working on: how much detailed analysis were you able to generate from these small amounts of material?

ARTICLE A

NIGHT SCENES IN LONDON

Big Crowds Visit Main Points of Interest

At nine o'clock last night and even at a much later hour, the wide pavements of Whitehall were thick with people moving in the direction of the Abbey, and the Strand too, was crowded and congested with vehicular traffic. There was a long queue leading to the Cenotaph, the plinth of which was bright with the spring flowers of Anzac Day.

Up to 7.30 there was a long procession through the Abbey to behold the altar at which were solemnised the nuptials of the Royal bridegroom and her ladyship. There were reverent pauses at the grave of the Unknown Warrior, on which reposed in its delicate beauty the bouquet of the bride. The Dean and Chapter charged a shilling for entrance, so the Abbey Restoration Fund will benefit to the extent of hundreds of pounds.

It was a homely crowd of people which clustered around the Abbey last night. There were those who [were] kept at business during the morning and family parties who sauntered along admiring the decorations. Buckingham Palace drew many sightseers and the Mall too, was lively.

ARTICLE B

London under siege as Royal Wedding fever grips tourists

ROYAL FEVER hit London yesterday – three days to go to the wedding.

The route Prince Charles and Lady Diana Spencer will take at St Paul's was jammed with sightseers and well-wishers, and the City of London, normally a ghost town on Sundays, was besieged by visitors.

Thousands of people crowded to push their way into St Paul's to get a glimpse of the scene on which world TV will focus on Wednesday.

Shopkeeper Brian Hinton, selling souvenirs outside the cathedral, said: 'London has gone mad. It's crazy. The city is bulging with people wanting a glimpse of anything connected with the wedding.'

Mr Hinton has had to turn away people wanting to sleep outside his shop and is staying open 14 hours a day to deal with souvenir hunters.

'Anything which has a picture of the couple on it or their names is being snapped up,' he said.

By eight o'clock yesterday morning more than 10,000 people were already lining the wedding route to watch a full dress rehearsal of the carriage procession.

Hours later, the streets were still filled with coachloads of tourists and police were having a headache dealing with the traffic.

'It's far worse than a normal rush hour,' said one policeman. 'Everyone is moving so slowly. I've even seen people sitting in their cars munching picnics.'

At St Paul's officials hoped to have crammed more than 15,000 through the doors.

'But there will be thousands we will have to turn away,' said an official. 'You cannot see the steps leading up here because of the queues.'

And in another part of London the biggest street party ever held was taking place because of the wedding.

About 5,500 youngsters, more than 1,000 of them handicapped or disabled, ate, drank, and cheered their way through the afternoon during celebrations in Oxford Street.

Lady Diana's nerves were put to the test again yesterday as Prince Charles took on the Spanish in an international polo match at Windsor Great Park.

Lady Diana, a bride in three days' time, was flustered and fretful on Saturday when crowds and cameramen pressed too close during a polo match at Indworth, Hampshire.

Yesterday she managed to keep her cool, but only just. At one stage she walked with head down and blushed hotly when detectives led her back through the crowds to the Royal Pavilion.

Lady Diana, who is said to have lost a stone recently, looked thin and rather pale but clapped enthusiastically as her husband-to-be's team beat the Spanish 10-5 in the polo match.

More Royal Wedding news - Page Five.

ARTICLE C

THE DUKE'S HONEYMOON

The honeymoon of the Duke of York and his bride will not be a long one. They will travel like any ordinary well-to-do young couple, without any attendants save a maid and a valet to take care of the luggage. There is great excitement around Glamis, where it is said that the second part of their honeymoon will be spent. Nearly all Lady Elizabeth Bowes-Lyons's childhood was there, and the people of the neighbourhood are as devoted to her as she is to them.

ARTICLE D

At sea on the Royal love boat

PRINCE Charles and Lady Diana Spencer will spend the first two days of their honeymoon at Broadlands, the Hampshire home of the late Earl Mountbatten, Buckingham Palace announced last night.

The Royal couple will fly to Gibraltar on August 1. There they will join the Royal Yacht Britannia and spend about two weeks cruising in the Mediterranean.

A statement from the Palace said no further details about the honeymoon would be made available.

The announcement ended weeks of speculation. Earlier reports had suggested that the couple would be honeymooning in the Caribbean.

✦ RESEARCH PATHWAYS ✦

Further historical comparisons of similar events, e.g. the Titanic/Zeebrugge disasters; study of particular news features, e.g. weather forecasts; study of how men and women are described in the press; contemporary news coverage of a particular event; study of a specific language level and its effects across a range of papers, e.g. phonological patterning, use of puns/metaphors in headlines and articles in the tabloid press.

Magazines

The magazine trade is a huge industry which caters for a wide variety of different groups. To get you started on thinking about the nature of magazines and the way they vary, try the activities below:

INITIAL ACTIVITY I or

What are the purposes of magazines?

Here are some suggestions. Try to think of one example of a magazine which has the purpose outlined, and add any further purposes you think are relevant:

To inform: To instruct:
To entertain: To persuade:

How do you think magazines differ from newspapers in the functions they fulfil?

♦ ♦ ♦

INITIAL ACTIVITY II or

How do the target groups for different magazines vary?

Here are some possible variations in audience.

Can you think of any magazines that fit the variations outlined?

Add any further variations which you think are relevant:

Different age groups: Different religious groups:
Different gender groups: Different ethnic groups:
Different interest groups: Different political groups:
Different social class groups:

♦ ♦ ♦

INITIAL ACTIVITY III or

The word 'magazine' is an Arabic word (originally 'makhasin'), meaning 'storehouses'. It is still used to mean a store for explosives or a supply-chamber in a machine (e.g. a magazine of rounds of bullets in an automatic gun).

Can you see any link between the original meaning of this Arabic word and the idea of a written publication? Does the Arabic word give a clue to the nature of the modern magazine?

Brainstorm the typical ingredients for one type or 'genre' of magazine: what features would a reader expect to find in it?

♦ ♦ ♦

FURTHER ACTIVITY I

Consider the following:

- Were you able to identify magazines written for different purposes, or do most magazines fulfil more than one purpose?

- Were you able to identify different target groups for a range of publications?

- How far were you able to list the typical ingredients of your chosen magazine genre?

◆ ◆ ◆

The activities you have just worked on should have helped you to see the complexity of the area of written language we refer to as 'magazines'. To try to analyse a whole range of magazines, or even one magazine, without having a clearly defined question in mind, and without a sharp focus on particular features, will mean that you won't be able to say very much of interest or value about the language.

In order to analyse the language, it is often useful to set up a contrast of some kind between different magazines with a focus on a particular feature. Then you can speculate, on the basis of proper evidence, about the purposes and audience for the language you have analysed.

To see what this means in practice, try the activity below:

FURTHER ACTIVITY II

Look at the two 'problem pages' on pp.129–130. Read them thoroughly. They are both from *Woman* – one from 1947 and one from 1987.

The problems dealt with on the two pages have some areas in common.

Make notes on the following language levels. Some examples of what to look for in each area have been given, to help you:

- *Graphological level*: How do the layouts, use of images, typefaces, etc. vary, and what are the reasons for the variations?

- *Semantic level*: What are the connotations of the different names of the agony aunts? How do their names, and the way they are described, represent their roles? What differences in vocabulary are noticeable in the two texts? Look particularly at the language used to describe behaviour.

  Do the agony aunts differ in how they address the writers of the letters (and therefore the readers of the page, by implication)?

  Do the two texts show any difference in levels of formality of language use? If so, can you find some examples of language to illustrate this?

- *Grammatical level*: How are statements and questions used to express meaning in the two texts?

  Are there any differences in the degree of certainty or hesitancy expressed by the two agony aunts?

  Are there any differences in how personal or impersonal they sound?

- *Discourse level*: Are there any differences between the whole purpose of the two texts? For example, are they both simply a direct question-and-answer correspondence?

  What does the language of the two texts tell you about any changes in society's attitude to relationships and behaviour?

  Have there been any changes in how agony aunts are seen, in *Woman* magazine?

✦ ✦ ✦

FURTHER ACTIVITY III

If you have been working in groups, share your ideas on the two problem pages.

Whatever your chosen working method, write up your notes in summary form under the headings given. Also consider the following:

- Do you feel that a comparison such as this can enable a detailed focus on language: how much detail were you able to go into, in your analysis of these texts?

- What advantage is there in having some of the subject matter in common in the two texts?

✦ ✦ ✦

FURTHER ACTIVITY IV

Taking a historical perspective on a particular feature is one way to achieve a good focus on language in projects on magazines.

Another possibility is to look at a particular feature or features across different magazines published at the same time but aimed, either at different audiences (e.g. teenagers vs. adults), or at the same type of audience but with slightly different beliefs and concerns (e.g. women of different social classes). In this case, you would be looking at possible variations according to some of the groups you brainstormed in *Initial Activity II*.

To get an idea of what this might entail, look at another problem page on p.131 – this time from *Woman and Home*, a contemporary of the 1947 *Woman* magazine on p.129.

How does the *Woman and Home* text compare with the *Woman* problem page you have just been studying? Analyse the two texts and make some notes as before.

✦ ✦ ✦

ASK

Evelyn Home

If you have a personal problem, there's a shadow over the sun. Let Evelyn Home help to smooth away the trouble—her address is c/o WOMAN, 186 High Holborn, London, WC1. Send a stamped addressed envelope for her reply

SEEING HIS WIFE

LOVE can be a cruel emotion, as cruel as it is strong. Its cruelty lies in its blindness—people in love tend to see only themselves, their eyes are closed to whatever misery may be given to others by their passion.

In a letter from a wife whose husband left her for a younger girl there is this sentence: "I loved my husband dearly, but it didn't make any difference to the girl—she broke up my family three months ago."

The letter continues, "He tried to come back to me and sent her away, but she would not leave him alone. She kept telephoning him and worrying him, until at last he went to her again. These girls don't know the heartache they bring—but I wish they would always try to see the man's wife before they steal a husband. Then they might understand how a women feels."

I think the only thing that can really put these triangular problems to rights is an influx of common sense and decency into the husband. He is primarily in the wrong—he has broken his vows to his wife, betrayed and encouraged a girl into loving him, and (in the above case) has endeavoured to retain the affections of both women without adequate return to either.

But love is blind. The wife is blind to her husband's weakness and irresponsibility, the girl is blind to the unhappiness of her future as the companion of a married man, the man is blind to everything but his own transient pleasure.

Supposing the girl did come to see the wife. To her, the wife would be nothing more than a woman who had legal rights over her lover—but no human rights. The wife would regard the girl as a usurper, an irresponsible flirt and a hard-hearted hussy. Could such a meeting and such points of view help in any way?

I am not laying down the law on the matter, however. In some cases, where the women concerned are more dispassionate, a meeting between wife and the other woman might be very useful.

AWKWARD AND DANGEROUS

We are very great friends as a family, with another family where there is a boy of my own age. This boy and I grew up together and have always been good pals until a few weeks ago when we went out together and were walking home.

He suddenly began to make violent love to me, dragged me off the road and I was terrified what would happen. Fortunately some people came along and I was able to escape, but since then I have been terrified of him.

I never want to see him again, and never would but for the fact that his parents and my parents are great friends. I don't like to tell anyone about it.

Tell your own parents about it, at once, my dear. If they are friendly with the other family, it need make no difference—but they can see that you need never be alone with this young man again.

If necessary, they could tell his parents something of the matter, but the prime necessity is to protect you in future.

UNUSUAL AFFECTION

A fairly senior woman member of our office staff has become far too friendly with another girl—a junior—and seems to be absolutely devoted to her. The rest of us feel that this is unfair to the junior, as well as being abnormal.

Is there any way in which it might be stopped? It is upsetting us all.

It is quite possible, you know, that there is nothing abnormal in this. A lonely middle-aged woman can strike up a half-motherly, quite harmless, friendship with a younger girl.

If, though, abnormality should enter into the case, there is little any outsider could do. The girl would in all probability find other friends and the tragedy would not be hers, but the older woman's.

As neither of these people has asked for help or advice, I can really only suggest that no one interferes with what is essentially a private, personal matter.

Virginia Ironside

'Don't just sit and worry,' share your problem with Virginia who's always here to help

Bitter news

I'm a single parent with a three-year-old son and his father comes to see him each weekend. The problem is that I still love him and can't stand the thought of his being with other women. I can't stand, either, the poverty and loneliness he has left me with. The resentment towards my ex-boyfriend has got so bad that I've started saying things to my son to turn him against his father. We also argue bitterly in front of him and I'm afraid I am getting confused. My own parents did with me. I was very unhappy so I know how awful it is but I can't stop myself, I wouldn't go to counselling or Gingerbread by the way, so please don't suggest this.

I'm sorry you're so dead set against seeking help—but I understand that it is hard to think positively when you're feeling so low. Still, you owe it to your young son to sort out this problem. Couldn't you kill two birds with one stone by asking your ex-boyfriend to take your son out for the day and have him for a night at weekends? This way you wouldn't argue in front of him, and you have some time and an evening to yourself. This is where Gingerbread would help, I have to say—you'd meet others so you could pool your resources and get out. Don't run your son's father down to him, whatever you do. If you do, apologise later and say that you didn't mean it. Small children can understand this sort of contradiction up to a point—but of course it's better not to do it in the first place. I'll send you my leaflet on single parents which has lots of addresses and sources of help.

Did he rape me?

I stopped going out with my boyfriend six months ago but last week he came round drunk and raped me. I went to report him to the police but my friend says that as I allowed him to have intercourse with me in the past, then this couldn't be classed as rape. Surely this isn't right?

No, indeed it is not and you should report him. I have to say, though, that as you have left it a while and you haven't got medical evidence, which usually needs to be seen as soon as possible after a rape takes place, you may find it hard to prove. Added to this, your boyfriend will obviously say that you were willing and, because you used to sleep together, you will find it harder to convince people he raped you this time. You will find support, by the way, from your local Rape Crisis Centre. The central number is 01-837 1600. While I'm on the subject, I'd like to correct what I said in February about a woman who consented to intercourse but withdrew her consent *during* intercourse. I said the man would not be found guilty of rape but in fact a New Zealand case has been drawn to my attention which holds that he would be found guilty. Whether one thinks this is right or not, this is the law which would be followed in this country.

Sexual fears

Until last year when I was 22 I was a virgin—simply because I was terrified of my 'first time'. I even thought I was gay—and had an affair with a close girlfriend which ended and left me unhappy. But I now realise what's wrong with me. I have a fear of someone entering me. Even with my girlfriend there were moments when I got very tense. I find myself turned on to men now but only if there's no risk of anything happening. Can you help me?

I certainly think you need to talk this problem over with a sex counsellor. The Marriage Guidance Council has psychosexual clinics and it's there you'd probably meet a trained counsellor who would be able to help you with your fears. You've got so far working things out already, you are intelligent and highly-motivated. This problem is not at all uncommon. I'll send you my sex leaflet which has other sources of help but the Marriage Guidance (under M in the phone book) would be the best, I feel.

THERE IS
A WAY—

*   *   *

Perhaps You Are Anxious About A Little Social Matter, Perhaps You Need Advice In The Choosing Of A Career; We Will Gladly Advise You. If You Would Like Our Help, Address Your Letter To: THE EDITRESS, c/o WOMAN AND HOME, The Fleetway House, Farringdon Street, London, E.C.4, Enclosing A Stamped, Self-Addressed Envelope For A Personal Reply.

I have just received what I believe is known as a left-handed offer. In other words, a married man has suggested that he and I should have a love-affair. He has not said anything about getting a divorce and, as he is in a good social position, I am sure he would not want to break up his marriage.

The worst of it is I am strongly attracted to him, and he is just the one man I should have liked as my husband. I am twenty-four and he is thirty-six, and the days when we don't meet are quite blank for me.

He gives me lovely presents and we have such wonderfully happy times together that I just don't know how to do what I know I should do, and that is to send him out of my life.

I DO not believe for one moment that you would filch anything valuable belonging to another. You wouldn't do anything like that because, for one thing, it would be dishonest. Nor would you read letters intended for someone else because that would be mean. And least of all, would you deliberately set out to cause distress—let alone misery—to a fellow human-being. None of these things is permissible, according to your code of behaviour.

But is there one great exception to all these rules of yours? Something which makes this code break down entirely—when you happen to fall in love with a married man?

Reactions to this very serious matter are sometimes not at all what they should be. From the very first, the wife doesn't seem to come into some women's thoughts about it.

Do you never say to yourself, "If I don't stop myself loving this man—and stop it here and now—there's going to be bad trouble for another woman and perhaps a clouded future for her children, as well as herself."

I am sure you are fundamentally a nice girl and it often makes you quite unhappy to think what a muddle you're in. But you won't give it up. You can't. My dear, a man who lets one woman down will let another down, because it comes from a flaw in his own nature, more than from circumstances. That very weakness which made him transfer his affection from the woman he married to the girl he fell in love with, is quite likely to betray him again . . . perhaps when you are no longer a novelty. If this were to happen, you would understand just how his wife feels.

So, I want you to draw back, here and now, with all the strength of will you possess.

Never mind if it hurts. Take the long-term view, and resolve never to be the thief who steals another woman's most precious possessions . . . her home life, her security and her husband.

*   *   *   *   *

NOT TOO OFTEN

How many evenings a week do you think a girl should spend in her own home? I am Secretary of a Youth Club, attend evening classes, and belong to a Debating Society, and I am also taking tap-dancing lessons. And now my parents complain that they never see me.

Is this fair? I am an only child and my age is eighteen.

IT is good for a young girl to have as many constructive activities as you favour, my dear. But don't forget the intense pleasure your parents get from just seeing someone young and gay around to talk and laugh and brighten things up for them. Don't grudge them two evenings a week, even if it means re-arranging your programme.

And a word in your ear: the girl who before marriage gets the habit of thinking a quiet evening spent at home intolerably tedious will have formed a habit which may well undermine the happiness of her own home, one day. So do take my advice for your own sake, too.

INTANGIBLE GIFTS

Mine is rather an unusual problem. The girl I am in love with is an orphan, and has quite a good income of her own, left to her by her parents who were both well-off.

I am almost sure she loves me but I just can't bring myself to ask her to marry me, as I earn far less money than she has and I am afraid of people thinking me a fortune-hunter.

Could any marriage possibly be happy under these conditions?

I HAVE known several supremely happy marriages in which the wife happened to have more money than the husband. And it would seem hard that the possession of a personal income should deprive a girl of happiness with the man she loves.

Money is a tangible thing, whose value can easily be computed, but there are other, intangible gifts you would bring her.

Marriage, a home, children, love, and companionship. What is the value of such things to a woman? Ask her, and see what she says, and the best of luck to you both.

FURTHER ACTIVITY V

If you have been working in groups, share your ideas with the whole group. Whatever your chosen working method, consider the following:

- Do you think the language of the two texts on pp.129 and 131 suggests that the two agony aunts have different personae? Give some examples of language as evidence for your opinion.

- Do you think the female audience for the two texts are assumed to have different concerns and attitudes? Again, give some linguistic proof for your ideas.

✦ ✦ ✦

✦ RESEARCH PATHWAYS ✦

Articles from different magazines aimed at the same interest group, e.g. gardening, interior design, music; the same feature in magazines aimed at different groups, e.g. horoscopes, fashion, in men's and women's magazines.

Comics

Despite the attractions of television, video and computer – or, perhaps *because* of these media – the comic is still as popular as ever. Nowadays, comics are more and more closely tied to their moving image counterparts from a marketing point of view: Batman, Star Trek, and Superman all have both film and written comic outcomes where each medium supports the other commercially; a renewed interest in fantasy films – such as the 'Terminator' and 'Alien' series – has generated new larger-than-life gladiators who are female as often as male, and has brought the conventions of the comic format to the big screen; and new comics have sprung up in the wake of the success of computer games. Even so, old favourites such as *The Beano* and *Bunty* still survive. What are comics all about? Are they just ephemera, unworthy of serious thought and analysis, or can we learn interesting things about society by looking at their language? This section will help you to start exploring these questions.

INITIAL ACTIVITY

Make a list of the comics you read as a child.

Do you remember particular characters in the comics you read? Why were they memorable – what did you enjoy about them?

What purpose do you think comics served, in your childhood?

Is there such a thing as 'the language of the comic'?

See if you can come up with a description of the comic format. Think about:

— the titles of comic strips;
— aspects of layout;
— the structure of the narrative;
— typical vocabulary which might be used by the characters;
— presence or absence of a narrator, and, if present, what the role of that character might be;
— the whole purpose of the comic story.

◆ ◆ ◆

FURTHER ACTIVITY I

If you were working in groups, share your recollections of your childhood comics with others in the whole group.

Were particular types of comic popular with you all?

Do male and female group members find that they read different sorts of comic, and if so, why do you think that is?

Do you agree on the purpose of the comic?

If you were working alone, ask six informants about the comics they read as children, and about their views on the purposes of comics, then try to summarise your findings from this research.

Whatever your chosen working method, consider the following:

● How far were you able to define the comic genre by its typical language use?

◆ ◆ ◆

FURTHER ACTIVITY II

Just as an interesting perspective can be gained in analysing changes in the language of newspaper and magazine genres over the years, so comics can be scrutinised in the same way.

Early comics were targeted at boys, but proved so popular that girls' comics soon came onto the market.

Look at the four extracts on pp.135–138.

They are all openings from stories in *The School Friend* comic. *Extracts A, B* and *C* are from the 1957 annual; *extract D* is from 1959.

Explore the language of the comics, particularly the following:

● The representation of the non-English characters, including the language they themselves are given

● The language and roles given to the English characters

- Representations of gender

- The language used by the 'narrator'

- How far the comics follow the outline you brainstormed in the previous activity

- Which of the stories do you think are derivative of the types of stories that would have featured in boys' comics? Are there any details in girls' versions that would not have appeared in stories aimed at boys?

- What do you think were the functions of the stories, and what effect would they have had on their working class readership?

✦ ✦ ✦

FURTHER ACTIVITY III

If you were working in groups, share your responses to the 1950s comics.

Whatever your chosen working method, write a summary on the following:

- How do the comic stories construct ideas about gender, race and class by their language use?

✦ ✦ ✦

FURTHER ACTIVITY IV

Now look at a contemporary comic narrative – 'Calamity James', from the *Beano*, 1992, on p.139. As well as looking back at a range of early comics, there is also a lot to say about a single modern comic story from a language point of view.

Read through the text below, and consider the following:

- 'Calamity James' features in the comic after a regular story called 'Ivy the Terrible'. Ivy is constantly plotting to cause havoc in the lives of all the people around her. How do the names of these two characters break stereotypes?

- On the other hand, how do 'Calamity James' and 'Ivy the Terrible' follow a long and well-established tradition of comic characters?

- What aspects of the 'Calamity James' story are familiar in comic narratives? What overall purpose does this type of story have for young readers?

- Examine the various aspects of verbal language in the cartoon strip. What else is the language being used for, apart from characters' speech? Make a list of the various functions, with examples.

✦ ✦ ✦

EXTRACT A

Foiled by the Silent Three

Betty Roland, Joan Derwent and Peggy West were the members of a secret society, the Silent Three. They were spending part of the summer holidays at Betty's home.

A GOOD IDEA OF YOURS, BETTY— TO REPAIR THEM

THE NUMBERS ON THE HOODS OF OUR SECRET SOCIETY ROBES WERE GETTING QUITE WORN

WONDER IF WE SHALL EVER NEED THE ROBES AGAIN?

In that pleasant woodland glade, Betty, Peggy and Joan were thinking back over their adventures as the Silent Three. On several occasions at school they had donned their robes to fight against tyranny and injustice. No one had ever appealed in vain to the Silent Three for help.

BETTY GLANCED SIDEWAYS

MY COUSIN GWEN MEREDITH IS AT HERONSWOOD SCHOOL, QUITE CLOSE TO HERE. THEY'VE STARTED TERM ALREADY, AND — HULLO! WHO'S THIS ?

GOSH! IT— IT'S GWEN!

BETTY! YOU HERE! OH, GOLLY, I'M IN AN AWFUL FIX!

IN AMAZEMENT THEY GAZED AT GWEN, AND AT THE UNUSUAL OBJECT SHE WAS CARRYING — A BUST OF THE EMPEROR NERO

I'M BEING CHASED BY A COUPLE OF PREFECTS. THEY MUSTN'T CATCH ME — RECOGNISE ME!

OKAY, GWEN. LEAVE THIS TO ME. I'LL USE MY SECRET SOCIETY ROBE

NOT FAR AWAY THE TWO PREFECTS — CELIA DAY AND RENEE MILLER — WERE IN HOT PURSUIT

LOOK! SHE'S DISGUISED HERSELF IN A ROBE. AFTER HER, RENEE!

IF WE CAN GRAB HER WE'LL KNOW WHO THE MYSTERY JAPER IS

EXTRACT B

The pupils at Madame Devine's School of Ballet were practising an original ballet consisting of gay street scenes danced round a barrel organ.

EXTRACT C

EXTRACT D

FURTHER ACTIVITY V

If you have been working in groups, share your responses to the previous questions with the whole group.

Then, whatever your chosen working method, do the following:

● Concentrate particularly on the language which attempts to represent sounds. How does it work? Would it work if separated from the pictures, i.e. would readers be able to understand what the language described, if they had no pictorial clues?

● Try to answer this by drawing up a list of all the terms on a piece of paper, and asking some informants what the various words might be describing. Individual group members should each ask one informant; students working alone should ask six informants. The results should then be collated, and some conclusions drawn about how this aspect of comic language functions.

◆ ◆ ◆

✦ RESEARCH PATHWAYS ✦

Comics aimed at different genders; older comics compared with modern equivalents, e.g. *Batman*; representations of race in comics; a comic compared with its moving image equivalent; parodies of comic style compared with their originals, e.g. *Viz*; the use of comic formats in other genres, e.g. advertising.

Advertising

It will come as no surprise that there is no such thing as the language of advertising, although there is a variety of linguistic techniques that advertisers use to achieve their common purpose: to persuade. While the features of language use in advertising may vary, then, at least the overall purpose remains constant.

While it is perfectly possible to analyse the language of a single advertisement in order to see how the persuasive function is built up by its use of language, some of the more interesting researches involve comparing and contrasting. As with other areas of language research, a comparison can enable the researcher to see very clearly, and to point out to readers, why certain choices of language have been made. This is particularly true where the products being advertised in the different texts are the same or similar.

One difficulty for the researcher is that, even if a comparison is the chosen route, there are so many advertisements to choose from: on what basis can any comparison be made?

INITIAL ACTIVITY

Think about some of the ways it would be possible to make a comparison of advertising texts for the same or similar products. Fill out the list below by giving more examples of advertised products in each case.

Comparison according to:
— age of target group: holidays
— gender of target group: cars
— social class of target group: alcohol
— ethnic group of target group: hair products

When you have exhausted your list above, move on to think about the ways that the various groups you have described above feature in adverts, rather than being the target audience. The way in which a particular group of people is used to sell products could be the constant factor that links your advertising texts together. For example, what products use images of children to sell to adults; images of women to sell to men; images of middle class people to sell to working class people; images of Black people to sell to a white audience?

◆ ◆ ◆

FURTHER ACTIVITY I

Look again at the comparisons that it might be useful to draw in a piece of language research on advertising.

Can you now see a number of ways in which you could achieve an interesting focus in researching this area?

◆ ◆ ◆

FURTHER ACTIVITY II

Look at the five adverts on pp.143–147, which are all selling Ovaltine.

Adverts A, B and *C* are from the 1930s; *adverts D* and *E* are from 1988.

Read all the adverts through carefully before you start your work, then try to decide:

1. Who is speaking to the reader in each of the adverts – what kind of person do you imagine behind the words? What kind of persona has been constructed by the advertisers, to speak to you?

2. Looking carefully at the language, try to work out how you decided the answer to question 1. What was there in the language to make you come to certain conclusions? Try breaking the language down into the five language levels:

Graphological level: Images, typeface, layout, etc. and their effects

Semantic level: Words and phrases – their connotations, their level of formality or intimacy, and the reasons for this

Grammatical level: Particular structures used, e.g. commands, statements, structures that imitate speech

Phonological level: Use of sound patterning

Discourse: Whether the whole texts are working in a particular way, e.g. imitating a specific genre

✦ ✦ ✦

FURTHER ACTIVITY III or

If you have been working in groups, share your ideas on how the Ovaltine adverts work. Whatever your chosen working method, write a summary on the following questions:

● What are the different techniques being used, in order to construct a particular persuasive voice to speak to the readers of the Ovaltine texts?

● When Ovaltine was first marketed, it was sold through chemist's shops, as a medicinal product. Is there any evidence of this in the older adverts?

● From your analysis of the data, are there any other changes evident in the way the product has been marketed over the years?

✦ ✦ ✦

ADVERT A

"*I look forward to 'Ovaltine*" says *Mary Glynne*

"I HAVE always looked forward to my cup of 'Ovaltine' at night after working at the Theatre," writes Mary Glynne, the famous actress. "My kiddies love it too . . . . and I always keep a good supply for them."

As a "night-cap" for ensuring sound, refreshing sleep and as the daily beverage for giving glorious health and abundant vitality, there is nothing to equal delicious "Ovaltine."

This complete and perfect tonic food is 100 per cent. health-giving and energy-creating nourishment. It is scientifically prepared from the highest qualities of malt extract, fresh creamy milk and new-laid eggs. Unlike imitations, "Ovaltine" does not contain any household sugar to give it bulk and to reduce the cost. Nor does it contain a large percentage of cocoa. Reject substitutes.

'OVALTINE'
Tonic Food Beverage

Prices in Gt. Britain and Northern Ireland,
1/1, 1/10 and 3/3 per tin.

P. 943

ADVERT B

An open letter to Mothers of fast-growing children

THOSE children of yours are growing so rapidly. The great concern of every mother must be that the growth shall be normal and regular, and that body, mind and muscle shall develop at the same rate.

Many children show a tendency to outgrow their strength. They become listless and disinclined for play. Their appetites are capricious and they are often weak and ailing.

Healthy and normal development depends almost entirely on correct diet and proper nourishment. Every particle of the material used in creating energy and building up the brain and body is obtained from food.

Growing children need more nourishment than ordinary food supplies. That is why "Ovaltine" should be their daily beverage. This delicious food-drink supplies, in a concentrated, correctly balanced and easily digested form, all the nourishing elements and vitamins that are essential for healthy growth.

"Ovaltine" is prepared from creamy milk, malt extract, and eggs from our own and selected farms. These are Nature's best foods. Eggs supply organic phosphorus— an essential element for building up brain and nerves.

The addition of "Ovaltine" removes the objection many children have to plain milk. "Ovaltine" renders milk more digestible, and therefore more beneficial. The nourishing value of all ordinary foods is increased when "Ovaltine" is the daily beverage.

Give your children "Ovaltine" instead of tea, coffee, etc. They will grow up strong and healthy—with sturdy bodies, sound nerves and alert minds.

"Ovaltine"

"OVALTINE" BUILDS UP BRAIN, NERVE AND BODY

Prices in Gt. Britain and Northern Ireland, 1/3, 2/- and 3/9 per tin.

P677

ADVERT C

Specially drawn by Fortunino Matania, R.I.

Great Builders of History
The Builder of the Taj Mahal

BY common consent the most beautiful building in the world is the Taj Mahal —the memorial of an undying love and the mark of the genius of its builder, the Emperor Shah Jehan. The passing centuries have not impaired its white gleaming marble, and it stands to-day in all its pristine loveliness.

Through centuries the Great Builders have permanently enriched the world with work of beauty and strength. Their work has endured, whereas even empires have often decayed and perished.

And the builders of health have also done work of enduring merit. Their mission has been to upbuild the health of humanity and increase the sum of human happiness. Among such health-builders 'Ovaltine' deserves and holds an honoured place.

This supreme tonic food beverage is recognised all over the world as the best natural means of giving and maintaining good health.

Prepared from malt extract, fresh creamy milk and new-laid eggs, it owes its supremacy to the quality and proportions of these ingredients as well as the scientific process of manufacture.

Delicious to taste . . . easy to digest, 'Ovaltine' is also a complete and perfect food beverage. It supplies, in unequalled abundance, all the protective vitamins and essential food elements that restore vitality and build up perfect health of body, brain and nerves.

Remember—for health and energy all day and peaceful sleep all night, 'Ovaltine' is supreme. It stands in a class alone—there is nothing like it.

'OVALTINE'
The Supreme Builder of Health

Prices in Gt. Britain and N. Ireland,
1/1, 1/10 and 3/3 per tin.

ADVERT D

THE THAIS DRINK OVALTINE FOR ENERGY.

WHAT MUST THEY THINK OF US DRINKING IT BEFORE BED?

Before indulging in any strenuous activity, the good citizens of Bangkok indulge in a glass of their favourite energy drink. Ovaltine.

In Thailand, you see, Ovaltine is seen differently than here. They actually call it the 'kick the day off' drink.

And, as Ovaltine contains the goodness of malt extract, barley and eggs, why not?

Malt extract, for example, is well known as an instant and long lasting source of energy.

Eggs are an excellent source of protein. And Ovaltine provides calcium in abundance. (Through both the milk powder it contains and the fresh milk you make it with.)

And, a mug of Ovaltine contains no artificial flavour, no added sugar, colour or preservatives.

Small wonder then that your average Thai football team insists on a pre-match mug.

Yet, despite the reasoning, it still sounds somewhat strange. Then again, if we think they're odd, what must they think we are?

Bonkers, probably.

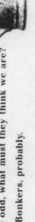

ISN'T IT TIME YOU WOKE UP TO OVALTINE?

ADVERT E

THE FRENCH CLAIM OVALTINE RESTORES ENERGY. IS THAT WHY THEY DRINK IT FOR BREAKFAST?

After a très fatiguant night on the town, what have this French couple headed straight for?

Hair of the dog, perhaps? Or black coffee? No . . . a cup of Ovaltine. Yet with the old joie de vivre obviously exhausted, why do they drink something to help them sleep?

Thing is, they don't. They drink it to wake up. Because your Continentals believe that the malt extract, barley and eggs in Ovaltine are a real boost to a flagging body.

Malt extract for instance, is well known as an instant and long lasting source of energy.

Eggs are an excellent source of protein. And Ovaltine provides calcium in abundance, through both the milk powder already in it and the fresh milk it's made with.

What's more, thanks to a generous helping of cocoa, Ovaltine has a delicious chocolatey taste.

Yet Ovaltine contains no added sugar, no artificial flavour, colour or preservatives.

So the moral of the story is this, girls. If a Frenchman offers you a mug of Ovaltine, beware.

He actually means next morning.

—— ISN'T IT TIME YOU WOKE UP TO OVALTINE? ——

FURTHER ACTIVITY IV

As well as looking at the marketing of one product over the years, another sharp focus can be achieved by looking at the use of a particular group of people, or at an idea or theme, to sell products; another approach could be to look at a range of adverts from one particular era for certain products.

Look at the adverts on pp.148–150, which all come from 1950s magazines. What main theme links them all together, and how is this theme constructed in various ways by the language used?

They'd found it at last—a home of their own. They were going to be so happy.
Then, things began to go wrong.

Jacinth was miserable...

so miserable she didn't know what to do. Only six weeks ago they'd moved into their very own home — the dream house they'd hunted for so long. Neat and complete, twinkling with fresh paint and new furniture.

And now, so soon, something had gone dreadfully wrong. Last night they'd had an awful quarrel because Derek had taken to coming home later and later from work — almost as if he didn't *want* to come home.

Why, he'd even said he wished they were still living with her parents ... how *could* he ... ?

The telephone! Perhaps that was him now . . . "Oh, it's you, Mother . . . Oh Mummy, I'm so unhappy . . . I didn't want to tell you, but I just can't help it. . ." Jacinth sobbed out her story.

"There, there, my pet . . . I don't think it's anything really serious. But, darling, I did notice when I came to tea on Wednesday that your house wasn't as fresh and sweet as it should be. Men notice these things, you know, even if they don't realise it . . . Perhaps Derek . . . Listen, I'll tell you what we'll do . . ."

That afternoon, Jacinth and her mother worked hard. Her mother had brought a bottle of ZAL disinfectant, and they put some in the sink, and the drains, and in the water they washed the paint and floors with.

"You see, darling," said her mother, "a fresh house with fresh paint and new furniture won't stay fresh and smell sweet without ZAL. Germs spread quickly, and that means smells. ZAL's so purifying—it's a wonderful disinfectant, and it kills germs at once and leaves the scent of real pines all over the house. I *always* use ZAL—haven't you noticed? I'll leave you the bottle."

A few days later, Derek, who was always home early now, remarked:

"I can't think why I said I'd like to be back at your mother's, darling. She's a dear, and it was fun being there, but there's nothing like having one's own home to come back to—and you do keep it so fresh and lovely."

Jacinth just kissed him, smiled to herself, and glanced towards the kitchen, where ZAL had a proud position on the shelf.

ZAL is the DISINFECTANT *that kills germs.*
ZAL has the fresh scent of real pines.
If you ever have a doubt, don't hesitate—
—fresh—fresh—freshen your home with ZAL.

Now look at these adverts, all from 1930s magazines. What techniques are being used here, to market this range of cosmetic products to men and women?

New Fashion in Face Powders
Makes Amazing Difference

The worst shiny nose and the coarsest roughest skin quickly take on amazing beauty when this new fashion in face powders is used. Scientific research has revealed a new ingredient which makes face powder stay on all day long. It is called Mousse of Cream. Blended with face powder it enables any woman to keep her complexion fresh and lovely in spite of windy or cold rainy weather. Even when dancing in the hottest ballroom it keeps the complexion entirely free from the slightest trace of shine and greasiness. Mousse of cream is now blended by a patented process in Poudre Tokalon. This wonderful ingredient makes Poudre Tokalon entirely different and gives amazing complexion beauty, impossible with ordinary powders.

A BRIDE AT 50

Happy Woman Tells Her Secret

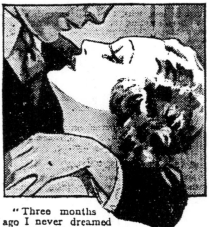

" Three months ago I never dreamed that a man would look at me twice. Anxiety and trouble had made my face wrinkled and sallow and I had almost given up hope when I read in the paper of a woman of over 60 getting rid of her wrinkles and looking 20 years younger simply by using Crème Tokalon Skinfood. I made up my mind to try it and to my joy and astonishment I could see my face actually looking younger every day. My present happiness and romance I owe entirely to Crème Tokalon Skinfood and I advise every woman to try it for a month. The results are marvellous."

Naturally this new bride prefers not to have her name and address published. Her husband is an important bank official and her letter can be vouched for. Crème Tokalon Skinfood contains " Biocel," the marvellous discovery of Prof. Dr. Stejskal of the University of Vienna. It nourishes and rejuvenates the skin; lines and wrinkles quickly disappear; sallow, faded cheeks become fresh, clear and youthful. By using Tokalon " Biocel" Skinfood regularly you can look at least 10 years younger in one month.

Your New Skin

White, Fresh, Smooth

Try This Specialist's Recipe

Wipe away those

Blackheads & Ugly Skin Scales

Latest discoveries now make it easy for any woman to quickly purify, soften and whiten her skin—no matter how coarse, rough and discoloured it may be. The new Crème Tokalon, White Colour (nongreasy) is tonic, astringent and whitening. It penetrates instantly. Thus, irritated skin glands are soothed and skin pores are tightened. Blackheads are dissolved and fall away. Wrinkles of fatigue vanish. The driest skin is freshened. An oily skin no longer shines or looks greasy.

When used regularly every morning, this new Crème Tokalon (White Colour) is guaranteed to give amazing new skin freshness and beauty, such as can be obtained in no other way.

♦ ♦ ♦

FURTHER ACTIVITY V or

If you have been working in groups, share your ideas on how the 1950s and 1930s adverts are constructed.

Whatever your chosen method of working, write a summary on the following questions:

● What differences are apparent in the approaches taken by the advertisers in the different eras you have been exploring? How are these approaches in evidence in the language used?

● The 1930s and the 1950s were similar years in that there was a shortage of marriageable men after the two world wars. Is this reflected in the messages given by the adverts? Give some specific examples of language use to support your ideas.

◆ ◆ ◆

◆ RESEARCH PATHWAYS ◆

Go back to the ideas you generated during the *Initial Activity*. Can you see, from these ideas, and from all the work you have done in this section, how you could explore advertising in a way that would enable you to achieve a detailed focus on the language used? Here are some more ideas: adverts which sell 'delicate' products, e.g. sanitary towels, condoms; TV adverts featuring particular groups, selling to particular groups, or using certain linguistic techniques; use of foreign languages in English adverts; techniques used on advertising hoardings; comparison between English and American adverts for similar products; techniques used in 'junk mail' adverts.

Written Genres

As an alternative to looking at language use within a particular written genre such as newspapers or comics, it is also possible to compare whole genres of writing with each other.

The aim for this type of study is to highlight the varying ways in which different types of writing work. Obviously, trying to characterise whole genres of writing by looking at many texts is an impossible task in a small study which requires detailed analysis, but small extracts of different types of writing can be compared usefully if the writing has some subject matter in common.

As an example of how this could work in practice, try the activity below.

INITIAL ACTIVITY

Look at the two texts on pp.157–158.

Both texts are about zoos, and are aimed at primary age children. The text in *extract A* is from a topic book called *Zoos* by Miriam Moss (Wayland (Publishers) Ltd, 1987), and would fall into the non-fiction category; the text in *extract B* is from a story book entitled *Who's For the Zoo?* by Jean Ure (Orchard Books, 1989).

Read the two texts through carefully, and consider the following:

How does the language differ between the texts? Explore a range of different language levels. Here are some examples of the ideas you could consider for each level:

Graphological level: How do the layouts of the two texts compare? How are pictures used, and do their contents relate to the texts in the same way? How are different groups of people represented by the images in the texts? What are the typeface conventions of the texts?

Phonological level: Is sound patterning used in either of the texts, and, if so, why?

Semantic level: Do the texts differ in the amount of information-processing they require – in particular, the amount of new nouns introduced? How are terms which refer to people and things linked together throughout the texts? How are different groups represented by the language used?

Grammatical level: Are particular structures used frequently in either of the texts? How complex are the structures used: for example, are subjects and verbs close together, to aid comprehension?; are active verbs preferred to passives?

Discourse: What is the overall shape of the texts: for example, do they have a thematic, or a narrative, structure? What purposes are served by the different texts, and how is this reflected in the language used? How would the books from which these extracts were taken differ in their overall organisation?

✦ ✦ ✦

FURTHER ACTIVITY

If you have been working in groups, feed back your results to the whole group.

Whatever your chosen working method, write answers to the following questions as fully as possible for your file:

● What general conclusions can you draw on the differences between the two *Zoo* texts in their purposes?

● How do any differences in purpose show up in the language used?

✦ ✦ ✦

EXTRACT A

Taking Care of the Animals

The people who look after the animals each day are called zoo keepers. The keepers start work early in the morning. They change into their overalls and wellington boots, pick up a stiff broom, a bucket, a hose pipe, some **disinfectant** and a shovel and go to the animal **enclosures** to clean them out. Then they prepare the animals' meals for the day in freshly scrubbed steel dishes. The keepers give a list of all the food they might need for the week to the senior keeper who orders it from the zoo's food store.

Penguins are fed by hand, by their keeper, as they will not pick the fish up from the ground. Each type of animal is given a carefully planned diet to suit its needs.

It is important that the animals are given the right kind of **diet**. Some animals need special foods to keep them healthy. For example, a vampire bat needs 0.25 litres of fresh blood a day and the apes like blackcurrant juice. The reindeer need a **lichen** that is imported from Iceland.

EXTRACT B

Chapter 3

Next day, Miss Lilly said that in preparation for their visit to the zoo they were all going to write animal poems.

"I want you each to write a poem about the animal that you've put in your picture. Before you start, I want you to sit and think for a bit about the animal that you've chosen. Think what sort of animal it is . . . what sort of personality it has. Whether it's a comedian, like a monkey, or fierce, like a tiger. Try to make the poem be a bit like the animal."

Cameron, who didn't like writing poetry, said, "How can a poem by like a yak?"

"Well, now," said Miss Lilly, "it seems to me that that's up to you . . . you're the one who likes yaks! But I'll tell you what, it's a jolly good animal for rhymes! Yak, back, clack . . . there are dozens of them!"

"Think how you'd feel." said Bader, "if you'd chosen gorilla."

"Yes, or hippopotamus," said Alison.

Miss Lilly pointed out that poems didn't *have* to rhyme. "We mustn't get hung up about it."

"But nothing rhymes with hippopotamus!" wailed Alison.

Cameron, suddenly inspired, said, "That's your problem!" and snatched up his pen. Soon everyone was writing hard. Miss Lilly said that tomorrow she would read out some of the best ones.

In the classroom at break they groaned at each other about the animals they had chosen.

"Hippopotamus is *aw*ful. There isn't *any*thing."

"You want to try *pen*guin."

"You want to try *pan*da."

Pavindra, always considerate of other people's feelings, said, "What about Catherine, with gorilla?"

They looked round for Catherine, but she wasn't there. Not even Soozie knew where she had gone.

✦ RESEARCH PATHWAYS ✦

Comparison of further texts from different genres where the content is the same or similar, e.g. holiday brochure compared with an extract from a geography textbook, both about Amsterdam: a piece of prose and poetry on the same subject.

Spoken Genres

Just as different genres of writing can be compared, or a particular genre of writing analysed for what makes it distinctive as a variety, so spoken texts can be treated in the same way.

The section on writing concentrated on the comparative approach across different genres; this section will look at one particular genre of speech: the wedding ceremony.

INITIAL ACTIVITY

Any genre, spoken or written, is likely to have a number of possible variations, and the genre of the wedding ceremony is no exception. Compile a list of possible variations by continuing the list of ceremonies below:

- Civil ceremony
- Quaker ceremony

When you have finished this list, read through the Civil (*Text A*) and Quaker (*Text B*) ceremonies that follow, and consider the differences between them.

TEXT A

Wedding Ceremony

Preamble

This place in which you are now met has been duly sanctioned, according to law, for the celebration of marriages.

Before you are joined in matrimony it is my duty to remind you of the solemn and binding character of the vows you are about to make.

Marriage according to the law of this country is the union of one man with one woman, voluntarily entered into for life, to the exclusion of all others.

Declaration

I do solemnly declare that I know not of any lawful impediment why I .... may not be joined in matrimony to

....

Contracting Words

I call upon these persons here present to witness that I .... do take thee .... to be my lawful wedded wife/husband.

In as much as .... and .... have consented to be joined in matrimony, and witnessed the same in the presence of this company, they are now husband and wife together.

TEXT B

Wedding Service

Suggested form of words

Friends, I take this my friend .... to be my wife, promising through divine assistance to be unto her a loving and faithful husband so long as we both on earth shall live.

Friends, I take this my friend .... to be my loving husband, promising through divine assistance to be unto him a loving and faithful wife so long as we both on earth shall live.

The service takes place at an ordinary meeting. When the couple are ready to stand up they say these words to each other.

Discuss the differences between these and any other religious ceremonies you are familiar with. If possible, collect a range of different ceremonies for further exploration.

Here are some examples of the aspects of language use you could look at:

- The purpose served by the language ritual that we call a 'wedding ceremony'

- How far the different ceremonies have fixed structures and utterances from which no deviation is allowed, and why

- The various statements, promises, etc. covered in the different ceremonies, and what conclusions can be drawn from any differences

- Differences in the vocabulary used in the ceremonies

- Differences in grammatical structures used

- The overall effect or message given by each of the texts

FURTHER ACTIVITY

If you have been working in groups, share your ideas on the differences between the wedding ceremonies.

Whatever your chosen working method, write a summary for your file on the following question:

- What are the differences between the various ceremonies, and how are these differences reflected in the language used in each text?

✦ RESEARCH PATHWAYS ✦

Further studies of particular spoken genres: for example, nursery rhymes, playground songs and other spoken rituals used by children; jokes; anecdotes; sermons; speeches.

4. Comparative Linguistics

Comparative linguistics involves comparing English with another language.

Data for exploration of this area is normally gathered from a speaker or writer whose first language was not English, and the purpose of the study is to compare the features and/or the functions of the two languages.

Features and Functions

Features are the 'raw ingredients' of language – the various language levels which were explored in previous units: sounds, written symbols, vocabulary, grammatical structures.

English may differ from other languages on all these levels, and the aim of a project on the features of different languages will show how they vary in a systematic way.

Functions are the purposes which language serves. Speakers who have more than one language may use their languages for different purposes: for example, one language may be used in formal situations, while another is reserved for use in more familiar and intimate settings; speakers will also negotiate their language choices according to the confidence and competence of the participants.

A project on the functions of different languages used by a bilingual speaker will look for patterns of usage, and attempt to describe the factors which trigger the use of one language or another. Switching from one language to another is known as *Code Switching*.

Bilingual speakers also sometimes mix their languages together, using words or phrases from one language in another. This is known as *Code Mixing*. Certain words may be mixed for the same reasons as those that trigger code switching between whole languages.

Work on Code Mixing may also consider the way particular words from one language are integrated grammatically within another. This will involve looking at the shape and type of words mixed, and their position in sentences.

Code mixed words may, in addition, be explored for their semantic content: are the mixed words from the same or similar areas of the vocabulary system, and, if so, why?

THE FEATURES OF DIFFERENT LANGUAGES

INITIAL ACTIVITY 🯅 or 🯅🯅🯅

Below is an extract from a conversation between a mother and daughter who both speak Afro-Caribbean Patwa. In the extract, the mother is talking as she moves about the kitchen, addressing her teenage daughter, who remains silent. At the beginning of the extract, the mother has found some jewellery on the kitchen floor.

The top line is a phonemic transcription of the speaker's language; the bottom line is a Standard English version of what she is saying.

Study the speaker's language and make notes on:
— her accent – compared with RP;
— her vocabulary – compared with Standard English;
— her grammatical structures – compared with Standard English.

hu	dɪs	am/mi	nəʊ	nəʊ	ʔaʊ	dis	dra:p/aʊt	ə
Whose	is	this	um/I	don't	know	how	this	dropped/out	of

dɪ	bɒks	jʊ	nəʊ/wen	mi	wəz	pʊtɪn	ɪn	də/səʊ	am	hæv
the	box	you	know/when	I	was	putting	in	the/so	um	have

tʊ	pʊt	ɪt	bæk	deə/bəfɔ	mi	get	lʊs	ɒf	dem/fɔ	ju	ʔæfi	gaʊ
to	put	it	back	there/before	I	lose	them/so	you	have	to

mek	kjake	fi	mi/enitɪn	dalɪn/aɪm	næt	fʊsi/mi	nəʊ
make	a	cake	for	me/anything	darling/I'm	not	fussy/I'm	not

pʊt	nəʊ	badi	ɪn	ə	det	mɪ	dɪər/enitɪn	ju	kən	əfɔd
putting	anybody	in	debt	my	dear/anything	you	can	afford

◆ ◆ ◆

FURTHER ACTIVITY I 🯅 or ⊙

If you have been working in groups, share your notes on the language of the Patwa speaker.

Whatever your chosen working method, present your notes in the form of an economic summary of the main patterns of language use you have found, by answering the following questions:

● What patterns of pronunciation difference from RP did you note?

● What grammatical features did you note as being characteristic of Patwa?

● Were there any words where you had some difficulty categorising the variation: for example, whether you should call the variation an accent or a vocabulary feature? List these, and explain why categorising them was difficult.

◆ ◆ ◆

FURTHER ACTIVITY II 👤 or 👤👤👤

Read the postcards below, which were written by a French student learning English as a foreign language at school to her English penfriend, Joann.

When you have read them thoroughly, make notes on the following:

- What aspects of English semantics (i.e. rules for choice of words and phrases) are causing the writer some difficulty?

- What structural (i.e. grammatical) aspects of English are a problem to the writer?

- Are there any aspects of English spelling or punctuation that are causing problems?

- For all the above areas, try to find patterns of usage, where the same feature occurs a number of times. Can you suggest how the writer's first language might be influencing her use of English?

POSTCARD 1

> Dear Joann,
>
> Thank you for your letters. I've just received it. I hope you and you family are well. Here, everybody is nice. The life is normal again: I go to school, I do my homework (which is not always funny) and I gave up eating too much ... though my mother is on a diet, she likes the sweats you offer us and so am I.
>
> I think you and your family are very nice to me. Now I'm going to write you something secret. I've been falling in love with a boy handsome for two weeks. The more I see him, the more I love him ... And what about you? I'm sure he likes you aswell. Well, I'm going to write in French because I'm fed up with writing in English (it's very difficult) and it's a good practise for you ...

POSTCARD 2

Hi Joann!

I think for you from the mountain where I'm spending my holidays very sunny and sportives. I hope that you and your familly are fine as well. I'm happy, because Tlasch is approaching and I'll introduce you my familly and my friends who would like to meet you as I talk about you.

See you soon.
Love Nathalie
x x x

POSTCARD 3

Hi!

I've just received your two post cards, it's nice to you. I wish I had come to visit you and your familly but when I heard of the date of the journey, it was too late. I had already plannified my holidays with my father otherwise, I would have come with great pleasure. I'm really disapointed not to be able to come (de ne pas venir te voir), because I keep a nice remembrance of you, your family and of the stay. It may be for a next time. As for you, if you want to come in France, there is no problems, you'll be alaways welcome. well thank you again. I'm looking forward to hearing from you. See you one day. Love Nathalie xxx

✦ ✦ ✦

FURTHER ACTIVITY III

If you have been working in groups, share your ideas on the patterns of usage in evidence in the postcards. Whatever your chosen method of working, write up your results in summary form. Use the headings that seem most appropriate to the data. Also undertake some research on the influence of French on the writer's English: ask a teacher or speaker of French to look at the cards and make some comments on the writer's language.

◆ ◆ ◆

THE FUNCTIONS OF LANGUAGE

INITIAL ACTIVITY

Below is some spoken data collected by *A*, a speaker of Punjabi, Urdu and English. The first dialogue is between this speaker and her sister, *B*, who has the same repertoire of languages. The second dialogue is between *A* and her mother, *C*, who is not yet fluent in English. Read the conversations thoroughly.

DIALOGUE 1

B: what's the tape running for
A: I've got to do something/for my English lesson
B: what/taping people
A: mm/I'm going to tape mum and dad
B: but no one will be able to understand it
A: I know/that's the whole idea/I'm not daft/you know
B: what do you want people speaking in Pakistani for
A: it's Punjabi actually/not Pakistani
B: alright then/Punjabi
A: it's for my language project/alright

DIALOGUE 2

The non-English words in the following are spoken in Punjabi. They have been transcribed using the phonemic alphabet. Underneath each utterance are two translations: first, a word-for-word translation, then a translation using English word order and idiom.

C: dʒɑ video tʃʊkæn
   go video bring
   go and get the video

A: film arndiheh
film bought is
have you bought a film

C: ah
yes

A: which one/where is it

C: television ne pitʃe
television from behind
behind the television

C: door bænd kar sardhi heh
door close it cold is
close the door/it's cold

Now answer the following questions:

● Why does speaker *A* use English in *dialogue 1*, but switch between languages in *dialogue 2*?

● Look at the way English and Punjabi have been mixed in *dialogue 2*.

  Is it possible to group the English words together, either grammatically (i.e. by their function) or semantically (i.e. by their meanings)?

● In Punjabi, verbs go at the end of an utterance. What effect has that had on the position of the English words used?

● Why do you think speaker *B* is surprised that her sister should be taping their family conversations?

● What do you think monolingual speakers can learn from looking at the way bilingual speakers use their languages?

◆ ◆ ◆

FURTHER ACTIVITY I **or**

If you have been working in a group situation, pool your answers to the previous questions.

Whatever your chosen method of working, do the following:

● Compile a list of questions you would like to ask bilingual speakers about their language experience, and try to find some informants to interview

● If possible, interview a speaker of Punjabi and/or Urdu, invite them to talk about their own code switching and mixing, and ask them to respond to your analysis of the Punjabi/English data

◆ ◆ ◆

FURTHER ACTIVITY II 👤 or ⊙

The researcher who taped the Punjabi/English data you have just been studying also collected some words of English origin from the speech of monolingual Punjabi speakers in Pakistan, during a holiday she spent there.

The words appear below, along with some details of how they were pronounced by the speakers, where the pronunciation seemed unusual.

The speakers all insisted that the words were Punjabi words, not English ones. Consider:
— whether the words the researcher found could be grouped into particular semantic areas;
— how the words came to be borrowed from English;
— why the speakers did not recognise the words as being of English origin.

yes		no	nɔ
1–10		please	
taste	tɛəst	thankyou	tɛənk
better	bɛtər	hello	helɔ
sit down		stand up	
tape	tɛp	cassette	
radio	rɛdiɔ	television	
book		copy	
pencil	pɛnsil	pen	
chips	tʃɪpɛz	apple	ɛpəl
biscuit	bɪskʌt	sweets	
police	pɔlɪs	door	dɜr
ice		nice	
paper	pɛbər	bag	bɛgk
cream	krɪm	lipstick	lɪpstək
brush		cup	kɔrp
bottle	bɔrtəl	town	dɔn
government		England	
London		cinema	
picture hall		like	lɛk school
number	nʊmbər		

The English language contains many words of Asian origin, including the following:

> shampoo bungalow kedgeree pyjamas gymkhana
> khaki have a dekko pukka

Do you think mother-tongue speakers of English would recognise these words as borrowings? Set up an experiment to find out.

❖ ❖ ❖

✦ RESEARCH PATHWAYS ✦

The language of bilingual speakers or writers in different situations or different generations; bilingual children in the early stages of language acquisition; the language use of bilingual speakers of different genders; original foreign language texts compared with their English translations; instructions, brochures, menus, or other written material which has been translated into English.

5. The Language of Social Groups

The area of language research considers how language use may vary according to the social group a speaker (or writer) belongs to.

Human beings are very social animals; we live in groups of various kinds. Some different social groups include the following:

- Age
- Social class
- Gender
- Occupation
- Ethnic group
- Region

INITIAL ACTIVITY

Think about the social groups above, and write some notes on how you think membership of them might affect the language that an individual uses.

✦ ✦ ✦

FURTHER ACTIVITY I

If you have been working in groups, put the social group headings up on a large sheet of paper, and underneath each heading write the suggestions of all the small groups. These are your *hypotheses* (your predictions, your intuitions) about how language use might vary according to social group membership.

Whatever your chosen working method, the activities that follow will give you an opportunity to test out some of your hypotheses.

First, read the notes on p.170.

Then look again at your ideas on your previous brainstorm sheet. What aspects of language did you feel might vary according to the gender of the people involved?

✦ ✦ ✦

Language and Gender

The term 'sex' refers to the biological differences between male and female human beings; 'gender', on the other hand, refers to the extensive social conditioning that makes us think men and women should be or behave in a certain way: for example, the fact that women can give birth to children distinguishes them biologically from men, and is therefore a sex difference; but the assumption that women are destined to look after children and clean the house while men are not, is a gender construction. Much of our picture of how men and women should be is created by the language we have to describe and talk about the sexes.

Research on language and gender can involve investigating either of the following questions:

● Do men and women *use* language differently?

● Is the language *used to and about* men and women very different?

Research can also involve a variety of different language levels. For example:

Phonology: Do men and women vary in their accents?

Semantics: Do men and women vary in their vocabulary, for example, in the terms of address they use, or that are used to them; in how they are described in different texts; in their use of swear words; in the popular phrases and sayings that the language contains about them; in the job titles that are used to refer to male and female-orientated work; in the personal names given to them?

Grammar: Do certain grammatical structures represent men and women in particular ways, for example, the use of 'he' to include 'she'?

Discourse: Do men and women talk about different things, and in different ways? Do men and women talk differently to their own sex from how they talk to the opposite sex? What happens when men and women talk together? Are whole genres of writing or talk preferred by one sex or the other? How are men and women represented in film and other media texts?

Semiotics: Do men and women differ in their non-verbal behaviour (their body language)? Are different symbols and images used about the sexes?

FURTHER ACTIVITY II

Read through the personal ads on p.171, where male and female writers are advertising for partners.

Do you think the men and women involved are using language differently? What are the differences between the ways they present themselves, and represent possible partners?

MEN	WOMEN
Tall, dark, intelligent, romantic male, thirtysomething, looking for a female soulmate into fun and intimacy. Love music, theatre, all things cultural. Hate macho and TV. You must be 18–25, slim, blonde preferred. Please send photo.	Sensitive, caring lady, 38, single parent, wishes to meet genuine male for company and outings. Can't do the Guardian crossword but willing to have my mind expanded. Genuine replies only.
Sociable friendly male, late 40s, no Clark Gable but presentable, good sense of humour, seeks female companion for good times and mutual satisfaction. Into eating out, films, travelling. Own house and car, good job. Just need you to enjoy the good life with me. You're 25–35 and not too tall. Photo essential.	Single woman, slim, quite attractive, non-smoker, 5ft 6in, 40, interests reading, films, music. Need quiet, shy male for friendship and maybe lifesharing. Photo preferred.
Professional guy, 31, interested in photography, music, clubs. Done scene and no joy. Want male partner for exploration of life and love. No one night stands please. Photo appreciated.	Bright, lively mid-20s woman, non-scene, seeks same for genuine relationship. New to town and meeting boring hetero couples. Rescue me!

✦ ✦ ✦

FURTHER ACTIVITY III

Now read the extract on p.172, which is from a 'Mills and Boon' novel entitled *Seduction* by Charlotte Lamb. The story is set in Greece, where the main female character, Clea, was to have an arranged marriage with a local Greek boy. However, the romantic hero, Ben Winter, arrives on the scene and attempts to seduce her. Clea is inexperienced sexually, and is torn between her need to please her father and accept the arranged marriage, and her desire for Ben.

In this chapter, Ben 'kidnaps' Clea from the beach after her early morning swim, and takes her to Athens for breakfast.

When you have read the extract thoroughly, make some notes on how the characters are depicted by the language that is used about them.

Clea walked on towards the gate which let her out onto a stony, dusty lane. Beyond that the beach began . . .

She swam for ten minutes, enjoying the salty spray which the wind flung into her face . . . When she came out of the sea she halted in surprise . . .

Ben was on his feet before she had turned away, his hand grabbed her arm, his fingers curled round her damp flesh in a grip which had no intention of being easily loosed. Startled, Clea lifted her head, her darting eyes wide, and met his little smile . . . She looked down at her arm. The enclosing hand, darker in skin tone than her own, enforced an effortless grip on her . . .

'Why won't you come?' Ben's voice had a sharp ring, the probe of his eyes fierce . . .

'Will you let go of my arm, please? You're hurting!'

His fingers tightened rather than slackened, the grey eyes turning darker, filling with impatience. 'No, I'm not hurting you!'

He hadn't been, it was true, but now he was, and she sensed that he was doing it deliberately, his fingers biting into her. She looked down, trying to control a strange trembling which had begun inside her, in the pit of her stomach, as though she had swallowed a butterfly which was trying to escape . . .

He opened the door of his white car as if to get into it, and Clea began to turn away. Hands fastened around her waist and she gave a muffled cry as she was swung up and round, deposited like a doll inside the car. Before she could get out again Ben was beside her in the driver's seat, the engine starting with a roar. Clea fumbled angrily at the handle as the car soared into flight, but Ben's arm shot out sideways and slapped her hands down from the handle.

'Let me out!'

'Sit still, and don't be a little idiot!'

She drew herself into a tight little corner, her eyes smouldering.

'You had no right to do this!'

'What have rights got to do with it? You wanted to come.'

'I did not!'

'Oh, yes, you did,' he mocked, his dark lashes covering his eyes yet leaving her with the distinct impression that he was watching her through them. 'You wanted to come as much as I wanted to take you.'

'If I'd wanted to come. I'd have accepted,' Clea denied.

✦ ✦ ✦

FURTHER ACTIVITY IV

If you have been working in groups, share your ideas both on how the male and female writers of the personal ads used language to describe themselves and others, and on how the male and female figures were depicted in the 'Mills and Boon' text.

Whatever your chosen working method, put together a written summary for your own purposes on the following further questions:

- Are there any similarities between the gender depictions in the different types of text? Give as many linguistic examples as you can

- Do you think the way men and women are described in fiction affects the way we see ourselves in real life? Give some examples to support your opinions

❖ ❖ ❖

✦ RESEARCH PATHWAYS ✦

Look again at your hypotheses about how the factor of gender might influence language use, and at the notes entitled *Language and Gender* (p.170). Choose one area, and try to gather some data to answer a question within that area.

Occupational Register

Different occupations all have their own particular language which employees entering that profession have to learn.

Obviously, occupational registers are not entirely separate languages, although some professions – such as the legal profession – may use some forms of written language which are very difficult for the uninitiated to understand. An example of such a text in the legal profession would be a Will, or a House Conveyancing Deed. In general, occupational registers may involve employees using commonly known words in a new sense – such as 'menu' in the computer industry, or 'poor' meaning 'not good' in the teaching profession; there may be uses of acronyms or other types of abbreviation, which assume shared knowledge by the users; whole structures of language, as well as single words, may be commonly preferred by people in the same profession; and there may be elaborated and detailed vocabulary associated with certain activities, artefacts or areas of experience.

INITIAL ACTIVITY

Make a list of some different occupations, and give one or two examples for each of words and phrases you think are used in that occupation.

❖ ❖ ❖

FURTHER ACTIVITY I  or

If you have been working in groups, make a whole group list of occupations on a large sheet of paper, and, for each occupation, write up the terms you found.

Whatever your chosen working method, consider the following further question:

● Why, in your opinion, do different professions use occupational registers: what is their purpose?

◆ ◆ ◆

FURTHER ACTIVITY II   or

Read through the example of occupational register on p.175.

When you have read it thoroughly make notes on the following:

● What *graphological* features are characteristic of teachers' report-writing, both from the evidence provided here and from your own knowledge?

● What conclusions could you draw from the *semantic* aspect of this occupational register? Are certain words and phrases used here characteristic of those often used in teachers' reports? Are certain terms used with a specific meaning? Are there words and phrases used that would be found less often in everyday uses of English? What does studying the semantic level of language tell you about teachers' professional concerns and preoccupations?

● Are there particular *grammatical* structures used in the reports? What are their effects?

◆ ◆ ◆

FURTHER ACTIVITY III   or

If you have been working in groups, pool your ideas on the linguistic features of teachers' occupational register.

Whatever your chosen method of working, answer the following additional *discourse* questions:

● Who is the *audience* for the reports?

● What is the *purpose* of the reports?

● Occupational registers are subject to *change*. Is there any evidence, from your knowledge of how teachers write their reports now, that teachers' occupational register has changed? If so, why has it changed, in your opinion?

◆ ◆ ◆

DALEFORD HIGH SCHOOL

SUBJECT	GRADE	COMMENT	STAFF INITIALS
ENGLISH	B	Janet has improved tremendously throughout the year, keeping up a very satisfactory standard of work and effort, and producing some impressive assignments. Keep it up!	CN
MATHEMATICS	D	Janet's lack of application this year has brought its own reward in her poor examination result. She must try to concentrate more in lessons if she is to make any progress. She is not doing herself justice.	EK
FRENCH	B	Janet has a natural flair for this subject, and has demonstrated pleasing progress this year, particularly in her oral skills. She could perhaps pay more attention to the presentation of her written work at times.	RS
SCIENCE	D	Janet lacks interest and motivation, working inconsistently and often handing in homework that has been hastily executed. She needs more determination to succeed in a subject which she does not find particularly easy.	PK.
GEOGRAPHY	E	Janet's performance in this subject leaves much to be desired. Much more sustained effort is required, and less willingness to be distracted from work. She behaves immaturely at times, and her examination result was disgraceful.	KW.
HISTORY	C	Janet is always co-operative and friendly. However, her level of achievement does not reflect her true ability in this subject. She has considerable potential, but needs to prepare her work more thoroughly.	WO.
TECHNOLOGY	C	Janet is too easily satisfied with less than her best. If she made more effort, she would be able to achieve a better standard.	Kmm.

✦ RESEARCH PATHWAYS ✦

Look back to your original list of occupations, and examples of terms from the *Initial Activity*, p.173. Choose one of the occupations, and research the language that is actually used in that profession.

6. Language Acquisition

Language acquisition is concerned with how children acquire language as they develop as language users.

Unit 3 in *Section A: What Do You Know?* will already have made clear some of the different aspects of language competence that children have to acquire. It will also be clear from that unit that the area of language acquisition is very wide-ranging, so, for research purposes, it is necessary to focus on a manageable and discrete aspect of acquisition.

One division that it is possible to make for research purposes is that between the *features* and *functions* of language.

Children have to learn about the *features* of the language system they are acquiring, i.e. the different language levels. They also have to learn how these different systems combine to form recognisable genres of *speech and writing*. As part of this process, they have to realise that the two channels of speech and writing are, in themselves, very different in the way they work.

As well as acquiring knowledge about all of the above, children also learn that language is used for different purposes, or *functions*: for example, to give information, to play, to persuade, to control behaviour, and so on.

Research on how children acquire language may take one or more of the aspects above, and focus on one child with the intention of showing how that child's development compares with what textbooks regard as the 'norm' for that child's age; it may compare children of different ages or abilities in order to account for different levels of achievement; it may compare a child whose first language was English with a child for whom English is a second language; it may compare a child showing typical development with another whose development is impaired for a particular reason. Groups of children may also be studied in order to examine the effects of social factors such as gender or social class; teaching material aimed at children of particular ages or abilities may also be examined in order to decide what the writers' notions of acquisition are.

INITIAL ACTIVITY I or

Read through the data on p.178, which is the speech of a child aged 2 years 4 months. She is reciting 'Incey Wincey Spider' for her older sister. Make notes on how far the child is able to produce the adult sound system: which sounds has she learnt, and which sounds are still causing her some difficulty?

Remember that this is connected speech, rather than words in isolation, so adults saying this rhyme may use features such as liaison and elision (see *Decoding Spoken Texts*, p.35).

ɪsɪ wɪsɪ paɪdə kaɪmd ʌp də wɔtə paʊt

daʊ keɪ de weɪ dɒps ɪn wɔst pʊ wɪsɪ aʊt

aʊ keɪ de sʌsaɪ daɪd ʌp ɔ də weɪ

ɪsɪ wɪsɪ paɪdə kaɪmd ʌp dæt paʊt əgeɪ

◆ ◆ ◆

INITIAL ACTIVITY II

Read through the conversation below, which is between three ten year-old children in a primary school classroom. The children have been asked by the teacher to design a board game. Originally, this game was to be based on their ongoing topic – 'Journey to the Centre of the Earth' – but the children decided they would like to design games for other classes in the school.

The children devised 'Market Research' questionnaires, and having collated this information on the computer, they now have to make the final decision about the type of game they are going to create.

No teacher was present during the conversation.

When you have read the transcript, make some notes on the following:

● What are the children using language for, on this occasion?

● What features of language mark the dialogue as serving a particular purpose?

A: Right, um . . .
B: Is it ready?
C: Yeah, it's ready. Right . . . so . . . what have we got to do now?
A: Right, we've gotta try and um . . .
C: The best one is skill and adventure . . .
B: They like adventure and skill the best. We need a skill and adventure game . . .
C: We could do a game like 'Hero Quest' where you design things like monsters . . . like monsters . . .
A: Gotta be skilful . . . yeah . . . so we gotta design our game
B: Shall we do it about our topic or shall we do it about their topic . . . that they're doing about . . . like skeletons and stuff?
C: Skeletons are more frightening . . . or shall we do sort of like polar bears and stuff like that or . . .
A: Polar bear, I mean, what?
C: Well – don't know . . . some . . . but sort of . . . aliens
A: It's supposed to be adventurous like chance . . .
C: Aliens are scary . . .

A: Skeletons we could do about . . .
B: That's not adventure and skill, is it?
A: Yes but they said the scarier it is the more they like it . . .
B: Yes, I know, but . . . I mean – you're not gonna have skill and adventure . . . the scary game and you say let's have skeletons stuck in the middle of a board . . . I mean . . . it's not very scary, is it?
C: You could search for the skeletons . . .
B: No . . . what you do is you have a game so you have a game which is really horr . . . horrific . . . that's like an adventure but you've got to go through and you've got to decide which one to go in like a big maze . . .
C: A maze! That's it! A maze game!
A: No . . . 'cos that's boring – not very easy, is it?
C: Have counters and you could make squares . . .
A: It's not scary . . .
C: You could say like miss a turn . . .
B: Not like . . . not like a normal maze . . . like a really . . .
A: No, we're not doing a maze . . . it's boring, that . . . think of something else
B: It's boring . . . how would you like it if you're just moving a counter up and down round a maze . . .
A: It's gonna be exciting . . . you could have your head chopped off by axemen
C: And you miss turns and go back to the start . . .
A: Wow!
C: And you get experience that girl said . . . remember . . . like that girl said . . . you get experience . . .
B: Shall we do that, then?
A: Well . . . I think we should have a vote
C: We don't need a vote . . . we need to des . . . why don't we design the two different ideas and the one that's the best gets done
B: Let's do . . . all do an adventure . . . well a maze
A: And decide which is the best . . .
C: Not a maze, then . . .
A: No . . .
B: Alright . . . an adventure game . . . don't shoot, don't shoot!
A: An adventure game and we'll decide which one is best.

◆ ◆ ◆

FURTHER ACTIVITY I   or

If you have been working in groups, share your ideas on the spoken data you have been studying.

Whatever your chosen working method, devise a way to present your findings in an accessible and economic form for a lay reader, so that patterns of language use are highlighted in analysis.

When you have done this, discuss what further data you could collect if you wished to undertake a *comparative* study of children's acquisition of spoken language.

◆ ◆ ◆

FURTHER ACTIVITY II

Below are three examples of early writing from different activity areas in a nursery school. The writers of these texts were all approximately 3½ years old.

Sample A is from the telephone area; *sample B* from the hospital reception area; *sample C* from the shop area.

Make notes on the following:

● What do these writers already know about writing?

● How far do the samples represent different genres of adult text?

SAMPLE A

SAMPLE B   SAMPLE C

♦ ♦ ♦

FURTHER ACTIVITY III 👤 or 👤👤👤

Read through the two stories on pp.182–183, which were both written by seven year-old children.

Make notes on the following:

● How much do these writers know about the structure of narrative texts?

● Analyse the writers' use of vocabulary and grammatical structures

● Analyse the writers' knowledge of spelling patterns: where the writers have not quite matched adult spelling patterns, is there any rationale for the child's attempt, in each case?

SAMPLE 1: THE TOOTH FAIRY

One day I lost my tooth at scool
that nihgt I put it aftr my pillow
and went to bed I'd forgotton my tea
Suddley a fant l'ght showed
it was marigold I got out of bed
and flew away with her and had tea
With her the hous was batiful it was made of
teeth then I went home

SAMPLE 2: PIRATE RED SHIP

Pirate red ship

once there was a pirate
called Pirate red ship he was
the leder and all the
crowe where called the
red ship and . they had
a red ship and
one day there was
a hyuwge crawd
arawend the red ship
the pirates were
going to sea that
morning but at night
there was a storme
and there ship surck
and they drawnt and
hide

♦ ♦ ♦

FURTHER ACTIVITY IV or

If you have been working in a group situation, share your ideas on the narrative skills of the young writers, and, of their knowledge of the writing system.

Whatever your chosen method of working, consider the following:

- How can you present your findings in a way that gives due credit for what the young writers have achieved, rather than what they have yet to learn?

- How could you conduct a *comparative* study of the development of children's writing skills?

◆ ◆ ◆

✦ RESEARCH PATHWAYS ✦

Look again at the initial notes on language acquisition (p.177). Choose one area listed, and consider how you could collect data for that area.

7. Speech and Writing

This area is concerned with comparing spoken and written language.

It will be clear from the material in *Section A* on written and spoken texts that the systems of speech and writing are very different in nature. But the channels of speech and writing are also very different in function, in what they are used for.

INITIAL ACTIVITY

Look at the headings below. Try to give six examples for each column.

What Is Speech Good For?　　　　　　*What Is Writing Good For?*

FURTHER ACTIVITY I

If you have been working in groups, share your ideas on the functions of speech and writing by collating your results on a large sheet of paper.

If you have been working individually, ask three informants to complete the same exercise for you, then collate the results.

To what extent are the functions of speech and writing different?

FURTHER ACTIVITY II

If you are going to compare spoken and written texts, you need to find situations where the *content* is likely to be the same.

You will have realised, from doing the previous activity, that we use speech and writing for very different purposes – so finding good comparisons is not as easy as you might think.

Look at the possible comparisons on p.186.

Which of these would provide good comparisons for spoken and written language use, and which would not?

1. A football commentary compared with a match write-up in the Press.

2. A leaflet from a DIY store explaining how to lay carpet tiles, compared with an in-store video explaining the same.

3. A recipe from a book compared with a recipe from a cookery programme on TV.

4. A teacher's delivery of a lesson, compared with her written documentation for that lesson.

5. A novel, compared with the filmed version of the novel.

◆ ◆ ◆

FURTHER ACTIVITY III

Go through your findings, taking clear notes for your own record, to decide exactly why some of the comparisons would not yield fruitful results – what would be the problem?

◆ ◆ ◆

FURTHER ACTIVITY IV

Read through the two pieces of data below. *Text A* is the transcript of a weather forecast from ITV News and Weather at 5.40 p.m. (items in brackets were graphics on the screen); *text B* is the weather forecast from the *Daily Mail* for the same day.

When you have read the material thoroughly, consider some of the ways in which the two versions differ.

TEXT A

(Today)/Hello/Good evening/well I thought we'd get things going by putting our weather into a European context/and basically all the action happens around us/now we're fairly lucky because the unsettled weather's kept at bay by the fact that we've high pressure sitting slap bang on top of us/

(Outlook)/so how does this translate into the actual/weather for Europe/and over Scandinavia it's very wintry indeed/a lot of snow/a lot of sleet/over the Alps too there's a fair amount of snow so at least that's good news for skiers/and really you have to come right down as far as the Western Mediterranean before hitting anything like decent weather/temperatures there aren't too bad/between 16 and 19/that's the low to mid 60s/the further north you come the chillier it gets/with Scandinavian temperatures coming in at well below freezing/

(Tonight)/well back over here for tonight now/and as the night goes on and the er clouds clear/well fog and frost very much become a problem once again/although in the south-eastern corner where there's a lot of cloud hanging on temperatures at least there will remain above freezing/elsewhere underneath all that fog a lot of minuses around/

(Tomorrow)/it's a sorry start to the day once again tomorrow with a lot of patchy fog around some of it being very reluctant to clear indeed and what with some of it even coming in as freezing fog you'd be well advised to take extra care on the roads and do keep those lights on/as the day goes on some of that fog should lift and thin/although it might hang on in the occasional place until the very bitter end/

(Temperatures Tomorrow)/so let's see how temperatures are likely to fare for tomorrow and between six and eight degrees on the whole/in Fahrenheit terms that's 43 to 46/and to confirm that high pressure/there it is settled over Northern Ireland/the winds fairly light though/(Tomorrow's Summary)/that's all from me/join Alex after the News at Ten

Reproduced with the permission of the Controller of HMSO

TEXT B

Weather

by the BBC's

MICHAEL FISH

A FOGGY and frosty dawn across Central and Eastern England but it will turn brighter for a time. The afternoon will become cloudy and there will be rain in most places by evening. Wales, the West, southern and Eastern Scotland will start dry with rain in the afternoon. Northern Ireland and Western Scotland will have some heavy rain and snow on hills. Most places will become windy. Rain almost everywhere tonight, showers in the West.

DISTRICT FORECASTS

1, 4, 5, 6, 8: Fog and frost at first, turning brighter, rain in the evening. Wind moderate or fresh south-easterly. Cold. Max 7c 45f.

2, 3: Fog and frost early, brighter for a time. Wind light south-easterly. Cold. Max 6c 43f.

7, 15: Fog patches early, then bright, rain from mid-afternoon. Wind strong southerly. Cold. Max 6c 43 f.

9, 10, 11, 12, 13, 14, 20, 21: Turning wet with heavy rain, but clearer with showers in the evening. Southerly gale. Max 8c 46f.

16, 17, 18, 19, 27, 28: Some sunshine, clouding over with rain late afternoon, snow on hills. Wind strong southerly with severe gales on coasts and hills. Cold. Max 6c 43f.

22, 23, 24, 25, 26, 29: Heavy rain with snow on hills, turning brighter with showers. Southerly gale. Cold. Max 7c 45f.

Channel: Wind southerly light, later strong. Mainly fair. Sea moderate.

AND YESTERDAY

Warmest: Isles of Scilly 11c 52f. Coldest: Tummel Bridge, Tayside –6c 21f. Wettest: Boulmer, Northumberland, 0.47ins. Sunniest: Tenby, Dyfed, 7.5 hours. London: Max: 6c 43f. Min: 3c 37f. Sun: nil. Rain: nil. Barometer (6pm): 1014.1mbs. Humidity: 84 per cent. Manchester: 1014mbs.

MOON AND SUN

Moon rises: 12.07pm, sets: 9.20pm. Sun rises London: 7.30am, sets: 4.02pm; Manchester: 7.48am, 4.02pm. Lighting-up time from sunset to sunrise. High water London Bridge: 5.16pm and 5.19am tomorrow; Liverpool: 2.22pm and 2.46am tomorrow.

AROUND THE WORLD — Lunchtime reports

	C	F			C	F
Akrotiri	S	24 75	Madrid	F	8	46
Algiers	C	17 63	Malaga	S	15	59
Amsterdam	S	7 45	Malta	F	23	73
Athens	S	21 70	Melbourne	F	18	64
Barcelona	F	13 55	Miami	C	24	75
Belgrade	S	22 72	Milan	R	10	50
Berlin	C	5 41	Moscow	C	1	34
Biarritz	C	9 48	Nairobi	F	19	66
Bombay	S	31 88	New York	R	13	55
Brussels	S	7 45	Nice	F	17	63
Budapest	F	11 52	Oporto	S	10	50
Cairo	F	25 77	Oslo	Sn	−5	23
Capetown	S	22 72	Palma	S	15	59
Casablanca	R	15 59	Paris	Fg	3	37
Copenhagen	S	3 37	Peking	S	15	59
Corfu	F	20 68	Perth	S	22	72
Dublin	S	3 37	Prague	R	3	37
Dubrovnik	C	19 66	Reykjavik	F	4	39
Edinburgh	S	3 37	Rhodes	S	21	70
Faro	F	14 57	Rome	F	20	68
Florence	F	21 70	Seoul	C	6	43
Funchal	F	18 64	Singapore	F	31	88
Geneva	C	4 39	Stockholm	S	−4	25
Gibraltar	S	15 59	Sydney	S	20	68
Helsinki	S	−12 10	Tangier	F	14	57
Hong Kong	S	23 73	Tel Aviv	S	25	77
Innsbruck	C	6 43	Tenerife	R	21	70
Istanbul	S	19 66	Tokyo	S	13	55
Johannesburg	S	29 84	Tunis	S	24	75
Karachi	S	29 84	Venice	C	18	61
Las Palmas	F	21 70	Vienna	C	7	45
Lisbon	F	11 52	Warsaw	C	5	41
London	C	7 45	Wellington	R	12	54
Luxor	S	29 84	Zurich	R	3	37

S-sun, F-fair, C-cloud, R-rain, Th-thunder, Sn-snow

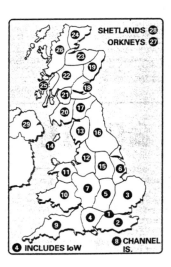

SHETLANDS 28
ORKNEYS 27

4 INCLUDES IoW
8 CHANNEL IS.

INFORMATION SUPPLIED BY
THE MET OFFICE

◆ ◆ ◆

FURTHER ACTIVITY V

If you have been working in groups, share your ideas on how and why the spoken and written forecasts differ.

Whatever your chosen working method, write up your analysis fully, using the headings that are appropriate for the data, so that any interested lay reader would find your ideas accessible.

◆ ◆ ◆

◆ RESEARCH PATHWAYS ◆

Go back to the list of comparisons in *Further Activity II*, and try to add further comparisons to this list. Choose one comparison, collect data for this, and analyse it.

8. Interaction Analysis

Interaction analysis (or discourse analysis) is concerned with how language is used in encounters between people.

The focus for a study of interaction may be a general one, for example, how the participants manage the conversation between them; or it may be more specific, for example, how a certain individual controls the dialogue by the linguistic strategies he or she uses.

Depending on the focus for the study, data collected may consist of one dialogue, or more than one. If a researcher wanted to compare the rules in different types of interactions, for example, the rules of a formal debate, compared with an informal conversation, more than one type of spoken data would need to be gathered.

INITIAL ACTIVITY

Look at the examples of possible interactions:

- A televised debate
- Children or teenagers talking in peer groups
- A teaching situation
- A telephone sales conversation
- A church ceremony
- Language use in a courtroom
- Language use in the House of Commons
- A radio phone-in programme
- Door-to-door sales conversations
- A family conversation

What questions might be of interest to a researcher studying the language use in these situations?

◆ ◆ ◆

FURTHER ACTIVITY I

If you have been working in a group situation, share your ideas on the questions that may be of interest in the study of the situations above.

If you have been working individually, ask three informants for the questions that they would like to see explored in the situations.

Note that there are no 'right or wrong' answers to this exercise.

◆ ◆ ◆

FURTHER ACTIVITY II

Read through the dialogue below, which is a transcript of a Brownie meeting.

Discuss how Muriel, the Brown Owl, controls the interaction between herself and the Brownies: what discourse strategies does she employ?

M = Muriel   K = Katie   J = Joanna   E = Elizabeth   C = Caroline
S = Samantha   L = Louise   A = Ann   R = Rachel   N = Nicola
T = Tawny Owl

TRANSCRIPT FROM A BROWNIE MEETING

M: Right Brownies, well just looking round a few Brownies tonight would have lost points and does anybody know why they would have lost points? For inspection we are talking about.

M: Katie?

K: Shoes?

M: Yes. Some of them haven't brought hats but some haven't got trainers on or pumps and you'll automatically be penalised and you will lose points. And that Samantha and Jane and anybody else and Joanna is because we can't have you running in shoes or sandals where you'll slip. You must have trainers or pumps . . . so will you, just wait a minute Caroline, . . . so will you remember for next week . . . As it happens we can't find the books and we're not having inspection tonight so . . . but for next week. Have you got pumps? Good. Have you Samantha? And how about Joanna, you've got trainers?

J: Yea.

M: Oh well that's alright then . . . fine, right would you just like to sit down and we'll have a pow-wow.
(Noise)

M: Right now Brownies would you like to tell me what you've been up to and where you've been on your holidays because a lot has been happening and it's a long, long time since we all had a pow-wow. First of all Elizabeth.

E: I went to Alton Towers . . . you know on the corkscrew.

M: Oh and what did you do when you were there?

E: Well errm we didn't go on the corkscrew . . . we went to, we were meaning to go to the circus but when it was time to go we were somewhere else dead far away from . . . so we didn't go and err we went on the ferry . . . and oh yes . . .

M: And what else?

E: The Magic Carpet and Michael started crying because he couldn't go on because you have to be a certain height and I could go on but he would have been crying when he came off it was awful.

M: Was it scary?

E: Yes.

M: Was it very high?

E: Well it was like that . . . like that.
(Cough)

M: Right Joanna, hands down the rest of you we'll give you all a turn.

J: We went to see my Auntie E . . . in the . . . and err she used to live next door to us but she's moved to live with her husband err in Wales and err when we got there we went to Rhyl and when we came back she started crying. Because err we went to see her because her husband's in hospital he's only got three months to live.

M: Err how old is he?

J: Err I don't know.

M: Not very old is he . . . oh dear. Oh that is sad . . . but did you have a nice holiday? Good, Caroline.

C: The best day of my holiday was my birthday.

M: Oh it would be. Tell us what you did on your birthday.

C: Nothing much because it was pouring down.

M: Well why was it the best day then? What presents did you get?

C: I got Peaches and Cream Barbie.

M: Who?

C: Peaches and Cream Barbie.

M: Is that a doll?

C: Yea I got a skirt, two tops, two pairs of knickers.
   (Laughter)

M: Right now Samantha.

S: . . .

M: Can you speak up love because I've got very bad hearing today. Where did you go to?

S: Chester.

M: Chester . . . Chester Zoo? Oh just Chester and what did you think about Chester?

S: . . .

M: We like it, don't we Tawny? What did you like the best?

S: The River.

M: The River, did you go on the river?

S: And . . .

M: And did David go?

S: . . .

M: Did he like it? Yes. Did your Daddy like it? Good how about Louise?

L: I went to see the Minster at York.

M: Oh.

L: . . .

M: Well tell the Brownies what the Minster is because some of them might not know what the word means.

L: Yea.

M: It's another word for a large church.

L: There was all . . .

M: It's like a cathedral. Good. Now, who's next? Ann.

A: I went on holiday and went to York.

M: Oh York . . .

A: We went inside York Minster then went in the Tower . . . down the road from the camp site was a little town full of shops . . .

M: Was it nice?

A: Yea . . . a penny arcade and they had all old machines in it.

M: Oh lovely.

A: And the lady let us . . . special coins to have a go.

M: That's right, special tokens. Now then, we'll move round this way next. Laura? Oh dear me, Rachel? I'm thinking of . . . right Rachel go on.

R: I went to the Lake District . . .

M: The Lake District? Was it good and did you get some good weather? No, did it rain? Oh dear. But you enjoyed it? How about Michelle? No, Elizabeth.

E: When we was walking back from the pictures we saw this dead cat lying on the grass.

M: Oh my goodness. Right I don't want any more tales of dead cats. Can we have holiday news please. Right, how about our newcomer, what's your name love?

N: Nicola.

M: Nicola, right Nicola you tell us what's . . . where you've been love.

N: Wales.
M: Wales, where about in Wales?
N: Somewhere in the middle.
M: . . . in the middle.
N: Yea.
M: Oh Mr. Jones, did you have a nice time?
N: Yea, it was my birthday when we went.
M: Did you go for the week?
N: No a month.
M: A month.
N: My Grandad and all my Aunties and all my cousins live up Wales.
M: Oh aren't you lucky.
N: Yea.
T: . . . Evans.
M: Oh Evans oh well that explains it. Right, what it is a lot of people live in Wales they are all called Evans or Jones that's why it's funny. Anyway Samantha.
S: . . .
M: Can you speak up love I can't hear a word.

✦ ✦ ✦

FURTHER ACTIVITY III or

If you have been working in groups, share your ideas on the strategies used by Muriel in talking to the Brownies.

Whatever your chosen working method, do the following:

● Decide why this conversation is humorously typical of those that arise in teaching situations – which particular discourse strategies are carried to extremes in this dialogue?

● Make a list of discourse strategies as headings for your analysis, then write a summary of your findings under each heading. Organise your work so that any interested reader would find it accessible

✦ ✦ ✦

✦ RESEARCH PATHWAYS ✦

Add to the list of 'speech events' you studied in the *Initial Activity* (p.189). Then choose one of the events, and decide what question you want to ask about it. Collect some data that will enable you to investigate that area with the initial question in mind. If the data does not answer the original question you posed in enough detail, are there other questions that are highlighted by the data you have collected? Make some appropriate headings for your analysis, and write it up in a readable and lively way.

Section C

◆

TAKING STOCK

◆ ◆ ◆

1. Planning Your Project

Project research involves a process as well as a product.

If you understand and carry out the process of research as outlined below, the product you create will be a satisfying outcome to all your efforts. The best pieces of research always arise from thoughtful consideration and negotiation between researchers and supervisors.

Poor research invariably tries to short-cut the process, avoiding consultation and not using supervisors as a resource.

The Stages of Production

Stage 1

Discuss with supervisor the area you would like to research.

Agree that you will collect some data by a specified date.

Stage 2

By negotiation with supervisor, decide on a clear question you are going to ask about your chosen research area, after careful consideration of the data you have collected. Select data, if you have collected more than you need for the question you are asking.

Stage 3

Read any appropriate secondary sources. Make notes. Remember that secondary sources are a guide to the area you are researching, rather than being the final word on what you should find: you may well find all kinds of details not mentioned by academic research. Don't be blinded by what textbooks have to say, and don't worry if there's not much written on the area you are researching.

Stage 4

Create a project plan with your supervisor. A plan involves setting up a number of headings for analysis of your data, so that you will cover all the areas necessary in as comprehensive a way as possible.

Stage 5

Consider permissions and confidentiality: if your material is spoken data, get permission from the speakers to use it; if your data is written material of a personal nature, ask the owner/writer for permission for use.

Stage 6

Write out transcripts, if the project involves spoken data; decide how you are going to present your data for the reader.

Stage 7

Write your introduction, explaining to the reader what you intend to do.

Outline the method(s) you have used to collect data.

Stage 8

Start your analysis, working through each heading in turn.

After completion of each section, check with your supervisor that you are on the right lines. It is not a supervisor's job to return your work 'corrected', but rather to give you feedback on whether you are analysing your data in enough detail. He/she may give you one or two examples of what this means in practice, then the rest is up to you. As you are working on your analysis, check that you are presenting your ideas in the most economic way: for example, could your findings be presented in tabulated form, rather than continuous prose? Keep your word count in mind as you work.

Stage 9

Write your conclusion. This should not be a repetition of large chunks of your project, but a summary of your main findings. Think about what you want your reader to remember, after they have finished reading your work – what is the main message you want them to take away?

Stage 10

Complete the final write-up. Check presentation, and secretarial aspects of your writing.

INITIAL ACTIVITY

Read through the stages outlined above, and look at a calendar or diary to see how much time you will have for your research. Prepare a list, under the headings *Stage* and *Date*, and put a deadline date against each of the ten stages to help you to plan your work. Keep this at the front of your research file.

2. Assessment Criteria

This unit provides a checklist of the general criteria that are used by supervisors when they mark research projects.

If you have past copies of projects available, it would be a useful exercise to 'mark' some of these yourself, in order to get a practical sense of what these criteria mean in practice. Whether past projects are available or not, it will be useful to ask yourself these questions at various points in the research process.

1. Ability to ask meaningful questions about language

Is the question you have asked a useful one?

Does it make sense?

Is it a reasonable question to ask?

2. Ability to arrive at and maintain a focus, purpose, and sense of direction

Does the project know where it is going?

Does it progress in a logical fashion, without being vague or going off at irrelevant tangents?

Does it stay on target, and keep the original question in sharp focus?

3. Reasonable scope

Does the project set itself a reasonable task, or is it trying to do far too much at once?

4. Good data

Is your data good for the question you are asking, or does it not have enough in it to enable you to say very much?

5. Open-mindedness

Have you been honest in the way you have collected your data?

Have you really looked at your data, or did you have preconceived ideas about what you should find, and therefore tried to make your data fit your foregone conclusions?

6. Rigorous, accurate and thoughtful analysis

Have you analysed your data in detail, or only commented superficially on it?

Have you analysed (i.e. said *why* the language was used as it was) or only described what was in the data?

Have you looked for patterns of usage in your data?

Is your analysis accurate?

Did you give some thought to how best to analyse your data?

7. Degree of engagement with material

Have you really quarried your material in your analysis, or have many things been left unsaid?

Have you shown enthusiasm for your chosen task and interest in the data you collected?

Were you motivated and determined to find answers to the question you originally posed?

8. Evidence of learning

Is there any evidence that you discovered some things you didn't know before?

9. Perseverance and initiative

If you met difficulties, did you persevere, and try to think round problems, or just give up?

Were you resourceful in how you went about your work?

10. Readability and word count

Is your style readable, clear and economic?

Have you stayed within the word count?

Has your project been presented in a way that makes it accessible to the reader?

11. Relevant and realistic conclusions

Are your conclusions clearly related to the project itself?

Have you claimed to have done things that you haven't?

12. High level of technical accuracy

Have you made many errors in expression, spelling and punctuation?

Acknowledgements

The authors and publishers wish to thank the following for permission to reprint copyright material:

Frank Martin for 'Black Wash', *The Guardian*, 15 August, 1984; Mike Fielder, Tony Snow and Trevor Hanna for 'Prison Guard Killed', *The Sun*; Oxfam for part of a 1986 leaflet; Granada Television for the extract from 'Coronation Street'; *Woman's Own* for the Old Bleach, sans egal and Zal advertisements; R. and W. Heap (Publishing) Company Ltd. for 'Shamed By Your Mistakes in English?' advertisement; James Lewis for 'Reprimand for Aids language', *The Guardian*; *Manchester Evening News* for the letter from Postbag, 10 August, 1984; American Greetings for the verses from the greetings cards; Owen J. McGarry for the verses and epitaphs; *The Star* for 'Night Scenes in London', 1923, 'London under siege as Royal Wedding fever grips tourists', 27 July, 1981, 'The Duke's Honeymoon', 1923 and 'At sea on the Royal love boat', 1981, *Sheffield Morning Telegraph*; D. C. Thomson and Co. Ltd. for an extract from *Beano*, 1992; Wander Ltd. for the Ovaltine advertisements; the Controller of HMSO for the spoken weather forecast; The Met. Office, for the weather forecast, *Daily Mail*.

Every effort has been made to trace and seek permission from copyright holders. The publishers would be glad to hear from any such unacknowledged copyright holders.